# FLIRTING
## with the
# BAD BOY

A BEST FRIEND'S BROTHER ROMANTIC COMEDY

# GIA STEVENS

Flirting with the Bad Boy: A Best Friend's Brother Romantic Comedy
by Gia Stevens

www.authorgiastevens.com

Published by: Gia Stevens

Print Edition ISBN: 978-1-958286-15-9

Editor: My Notes in the Margins

V072523

This is a work of fiction. Names, characters, places, and incidents either are the products of the author's imagination or are used fictitiously. Any resemblance to actual persons, living or dead, business, companies, events, or locales is entirely coincidental.

*While writing this book I learned what STFUATTDLAGG stands for,*
*so enjoy and you're welcome.*

While this story is a romantic comedy there may be situations that are triggering to some. For a list of those triggers please visit my website.

## CHAPTER ONE

# WHERE'S THE SPARK?

*Olivia*

His mouth skates down the side of my neck, nipping and sucking on my heated skin on his way down. I throw my head back only to be met with the solid wood door. I wince.

*That's going to leave a bruise.*

He pulls away just enough that his warm breath replaces his mouth. "You alright?"

"Yeah. Yeah. Just don't stop." My words come out in breathy pants. I turn my head to give him better access as my hands comb through his short dark locks. My fingers grip around the longer, silky strands at the top and tug, guiding him to where I want him.

*How in the hell is his hair so soft?*

I comb my fingers through his hair again. With our lips

1

still touching a fraction, I mumble, "What kind of conditioner do you use?"

He freezes then pulls away, eyebrows drawn together. "You're asking me about conditioner right now?"

"Fine. But it's so soft and smooth. You have to tell me later." I clutch a handful of his strands, my nails scraping his scalp.

He groans. "I love when you get rough with me." His hot breath, a whisper across my skin, causes a ripple of goosebumps in their wake.

"Shut up and kiss me." My grip on his hair tightens. I lift my knee to hike my leg up, but my shoe is like Velcro from whatever is sticky on the floor. I pinch my eyes shut.

*Don't think about whatever is stuck on the bottom of your hot pink Jimmy Choos.*

"You don't have to tell me twice." Instantly, his lips are on mine, demanding and punishing … and all wrong. I reach for his hand and place it on my cotton covered breast. He gets the hint and takes over, kneading the soft flesh over my shirt. I exhale a small whimper from his touch. My body grinds against his, needing any sort of friction it can get.

A rattle of the doorknob followed by a knock startles us.

"Hey, man. Some of us need to use the restroom." A voice sounds from the other side of the door.

"It's occupied!" Trey yells before going back to kissing the side of my neck.

*Bang. Bang. Bang.*

"There's three stalls in there!" the voice on the other side yells.

Trey huffs. "They're all occupied."

"Whatever, man," the guy on the other side of the door says.

"Now, where were we?" His mouths starts to descend toward mine again, but I put my hand up, halting him and causing his lips to crash into my palm.

"This isn't working."

*Maybe I need to be the one in control?*

I sigh and grab his shoulders and twist him around. With all my weight, I shove him against the door. Stretching up on my tippy toes, I press a firm kiss to his lips. His hands snake around my waist and his fingertips dig into my denim covered ass, hauling me closer. I rub against him, searching for the same pleasure I get from an eight hundred thread count mulberry silk sheet. But sadly, the sheet might turn me on more.

With a sigh, I pull away. "Do you feel that?"

His eyelids open slowly before he glances down at the bulge in his jeans. When his gaze meets mine, uncertainty is written on his face. "I think so?"

"Goddammit Trey. Not that." I smack his bicep. "The spark. Do you feel a spark?" I throw my hands in the air in aggravation.

Trey glances down at his crotch again, then up to me. "Uh … I don't know what you want me to say."

I huff and step away from him. On paper, he's the one I should be with. He's sexy as hell, confident, cocky, but not too cocky, and we both like sex. Well, we've never had sex together, but if we can't get past this kissing part, how are we supposed to get to the sex? Our chemistry should be explosive, like the grand finale of a Fourth of July firework celebration, instead it's a dud. You light the wick, but nothing happens. No oohs and ahhhs. No one likes those. Over the past two years, we've danced around this attraction to each other. Finally, when we act on it, there's nothing. Maybe we've spent too much time building it up? The anticipation is greater than the act. My blue eyes meet his steely gray ones and I make one more attempt. I place my palms on both sides of his face and bring his lips to mine. Once they connect, I feel … absolutely nothing.

Pulling away, I turn and pace the small bathroom. "What's wrong? Why don't I feel anything? There's no spark. And I need a spark. I need to feel something." When I twist around to continue to walk the other way, my gaze meets Trey's and I sigh. Maybe it's because we're kissing in the men's bathroom at a dive bar.

"Why did you pick this place?"

"Because we can't go to either one of our houses in case one of our friends drove by or showed up unannounced. All the hotels are booked for the tourist season. Too many people know us at Porter's. This is pretty much the only place where no one gives a shit."

"Ugh. Fine." I eye him up and down. He is everything I should want. But I don't. "Sorry, Trey. I'm just not feeling it."

His gaze casts downward for a moment before meeting mine. "Hey, it's alright. It would be better if you felt something, but I get it." He wraps his arm around my shoulder as he pulls me in for a tight hug. "We'll always have the men's bathroom at The Blue Anchor."

We both chuckle before I pull away, gliding past him and toward the sink. Careful not to touch anything, I check my hair and make-up in the mirror. When I'm done, I turn around.

"Shall we?" Trey unhooks the latch and pulls open the door. I take a few steps and pause, lifting my shoe to inspect the bottom. A glob of bright green gum is smooshed to the bottom. I groan. Trey eyes me suspiciously as I pass through the open door.

"There's gum on the bottom of my nine-hundred-dollar Jimmy Choos." I snarl my lip.

"Be lucky it's only gum. I've seen much worse come out of this bathroom," Trey quips as he follows close behind me.

"Finally," the guy from earlier says as we walk past him in the dimly lit hallway.

"It's all yours, man," Trey replies.

"What the fuck? There's no one else in here." We hear the guy yell as he slams the door shut.

Before we reach the end of the hallway, Trey tugs on my hand, halting my progress. "I'm going to get out of here. My ego can only take getting turned down once in a night. I'm going to go home and lick my wounds."

I purse my lips and tilt my head. "Or you're going to Porter's to find a girl to lick them for you."

"I can neither confirm nor deny any of that." He wiggles his eyebrows. "Want me to walk you out?"

I pause to think about his question for a moment. Sitting in the half empty bar with a drink sounds better than going home alone right now. "Actually, I'm going to stay and lick my own wounds."

Trey scans the partial view of the full bar that isn't blocked by a wall. "This doesn't seem like your kinda place to throw one back."

"Good. Then no one I know can see me wallow in self-pity. But you go ahead. We'll talk later." I stretch up on my tippy toes and place a chaste kiss on his cheek. Trey nods before he strides along the far wall and out the exit.

My shoulders slump as I stroll over to the front of the building where the bar is located. *When did this happen? When did I become the girl who lost her spark? And how the hell am I going to find it?*

Most of the stools along the long, worn wood bar are empty, but there are a few people seated while they drink their bottled beer and stare at the tv screens that hang on

5

either end of the bar. I find an empty stool, plop down, and wave the bartender over.

A man in his mid-fifties with salt and pepper hair and a full beard with the same coloring stops in front of me. He tosses half of the bar towel over one shoulder and narrows his eyes at me.

"I'll have a cosmopolitan. No ice."

The bartender crosses his arms over his chest. "We have beer or light beer." His voice is deep, and raspy, like he smoked a few too many cigarettes.

"Oh. I guess I'll have a light beer please. With two olives." I hold up two fingers.

"We don't have olives," he deadpans.

I drop my hand. "No olives then." I watch him as he takes a few steps and pulls out a bottle of beer from the cooler. He twists off the cap and tosses it into a bucket under the bar. He grabs a cardboard coaster and sets it down in front of me before placing the beer on top. Then he walks away without saying another word.

*People are really chatty here.*

"What kind of bar has only two kinds of beer and no olives?" I mumble. My fingers grip the cool bottle and bring it up to my lips for a drink. "I'm kind of feeling the three strikes you're out vibe right now. No cosmopolitan. Strike. No olives. Strike. And the biggest one … no spark. Shit. That's three. Alright, new rules. Four strikes. Or maybe one of those can be a ball."

I pick up my beer for another drink, then turn to the guy next to me. If I had to guess, he's mid-thirties. Possibly forties. Certainly, the youngest out of everyone here. With the scruff along his chiseled jaw and his dark locks loosely pulled into a man bun gives him a rugged, mountain man look. All he's missing is the red flannel shirt, and I'd be tempted to climb him like a lumberjack scales a tree. The

6

dirt under his nails confirms he works hard for the beer that sits in front of him. Definitely not the suit and tie I'm used to, but attractive nonetheless. Everything about him screams, bad boy. Maybe it's time I start being a little bad.

When my gaze locks on to his, a flutter erupts in my belly, and I blurt out the first thing that comes to mind, "Kiss me."

## CHAPTER TWO

# NOT MY TYPE

## *Ledger*

When I stroll through the door of the Blue Anchor, the place is like a ghost town. Just a couple of regulars sitting at the bar, and they mostly keep to themselves. It's the perfect spot to have a few hours to myself without having to answer to anyone. After the day I've had, I just want to be left alone. I sidle up to the bar and give Rusty, the owner, a head nod. I've been coming here since I was an eighteen-year-old with a fake I.D. Back then I thought I was tough shit, but in reality I was carrying around the fakest damn I.D. I've ever seen. But Rusty let it slide and I continued to come here even well after I turned twenty-one. He was always don't ask, don't tell and I sure as hell wasn't going to tell.

Rusty sets a beer down in front of me before he moves

on to the next customer at the other end of the bar. I pick up the bottle and once the beer hits my taste buds, a little bit of the day's worries wash away. First, one of my mechanics called in, then I received the wrong parts for a custom chopper I've been working on. The phone was constantly ringing. Everyone who stopped in needed something, and they needed it done yesterday. I was over today's bullshit.

The screech of metal scraping across worn linoleum draws my attention. A woman with blonde hair throws herself onto the stool and sets her purse on the bar top. Then she thinks better of it and rests it in her lap. Out of all the empty stools lined up along the bar, I have no fucking clue why she's picked the one next to me. I guarantee you I'm not radiating come talk to me vibes.

I do my best to tune her out as Rusty gets her a beer, but I have to bite back my laughter when she asks for olives at The Blue Anchor. Rusty keeps the drinks simple here. Beer and light beer, though he's tried to get rid of that one. Whiskey. Vodka. Bourbon. And you better like those on the rocks because mixers are as scarce as olives.

Sadly, once she gets her drink it only makes her more talkative. She rambles on about the olives and sparks and I have no fucking idea what she's talking about. I glance to my right and out of the three people sitting at this bar of twenty or so empty stools, she sat in the one right next to me. Well, aren't I just fucking lucky. I shift my gaze to the left and give her a once over. She's hot, blonde hair that falls past her shoulders, but one thing is out of place … her clothes are way too fucking fancy for a place like this. I return my attention to the tv in front of me, lift the bottle, bring it to my lips, and take a big gulp. Maybe if I pretend she isn't there, she'll go away.

"Kiss me."

*Did I hear her correctly?*

Slowly, I turn my head toward her. I'm greeted with topaz blue eyes. Even in the dim lighting, they sparkle. Her voice is sugary sweet, just as I suspected. I don't do sugary. Or sweet. "Did you just ask me to kiss you?" I tip up an eyebrow at her, wanting confirmation that I heard her correctly.

"Yes. I need to know if I'm broken."

Again, I give her another questioning eyebrow.

She sits up straighter on her stool. "Have you ever kissed someone and there was no spark?"

"Uh. No."

"Of course, you haven't." Her shoulders deflate. "You're a guy. Guys care about one thing ..." She glances down at my denim covered crotch, but the way her eyes linger doesn't go unnoticed.

"I could say the same thing about you." I peer down at my crotch, then meet her eyes. She says nothing, just lifts her beer and takes a sip. I wasn't expecting her to give up so fast. I figured it would take a little more than her getting caught red-handed checking me out to get her to keep quiet. Grabbing my beer, I take a celebratory gulp.

She places her beer on the bar, then swivels her stool so she's fully facing me. "I just need you to kiss me."

I choke on my beer as I fight not to spray it all over the bar top. As soon as I finish coughing, I turn to her. She's not going to give up.

She inches closer to the edge of her seat. Her knees almost touching my thigh. "Kiss me. I need to know that whatever I'm feeling is just a rut, and I'm not broken."

"Where I come from, we don't ask. If we want to kiss someone, we just do it."

She gives me an exasperated sigh. "I don't go around just kissing random strangers."

"And this is … what?"

"This is an experiment. So don't worry about that." She waves me off.

I bark out a laugh. For the second time in our brief conversation, she made me laugh. It's a foreign sound as of late. What is she doing to me? I shake it off. "So, now you're just using me?"

Her lips tip up into a smile. "For experimental purposes. You're not really my type."

I scoff. But truth be told, I'm hypnotized by her plump cherry red lips and curious how they would feel pressed against mine. "Wow. An insult on top of using me. How could anyone turn down your offer? I'll let you in on a little secret." I lean toward her so my face is inches from her cheek. She smells sweet and rich, like jasmine. I regain my train of thought and whisper, "You're not really my type either, duchess." I pull away while keeping my eyes trained on hers, wanting to catch her reaction. Her breath hitches. Then she squares her shoulders as she composes herself.

"My name's not duchess. It's Oli—"

"Don't care." I take a drink of my beer.

"Well, there's no reason to be rude about it. All I want is one simple little favor." She pinches her fingers centimeters apart in front of her. "Just a kiss. It's not like I was asking you to father my children. Also, just so we're clear, I wouldn't want that," she glances down at my crotch again, "anywhere near me."

I huff out a laugh. "I guarantee you'll be thinking about this later tonight." I nod toward my lap. "You'll be squirming on top of your expensive as hell silk sheets wishing I was there to take away the ache between your legs."

Her nostrils flare as she narrows her eyes. "How dare you make assumptions about me? You know nothing about me. Hell, you don't even want to know my name. You just think you're some big gruff guy, with a sexy bad boy vibe, and all the women will just flock to you like a seagull to a french fry. Well, guess what? That's all you are. A seagull."

"Did you just compare me to a bird?" I raise an eyebrow.

Without missing a beat, she replies, "I did. Because you're annoying with a cocky attitude."

"You're the one who sat down next to me and rambled on about kissing me."

"Clearly, it was a big mistake. The last thing I would want is a limp kiss from you. And I'm sure something else would hold the same limpness." Her eyebrows raise as she nods to my crotch again.

"You're on a roll. Now you challenge my manhood?"

She shrugs a shoulder. "I call it like I see it."

I lean in, my voice low. "Well duchess, I guarantee you I'd have you moaning my name in under five seconds. But I'd hate to dirty up your perfect good girl persona."

"Good thing we're not on a first name basis so I can't moan anything. And once again my name isn't duchess. What is it with guys and pet names? Is it so you can call all the girls the same name, so you never have to remember their real—"

Done with this conversation, I'll give her what she wants and grease covered hands be damned. I wrap one hand around the nape of her neck and haul her to me. Her eyebrows shoot to her hairline in surprise, and I slam my lips to hers. Nothing about this kiss is innocent and sweet. And whatever the spark is she rambled on about, I feel it. All the way to my toes and fuck, I haven't felt this in a long time. I pull away, breaking the kiss. Slowly, her long, dark eyelashes flutter open. Lust swirls in her irises, and I know she's found exactly what she's been looking for.

"Son of a bitch," she mutters under her breath as she presses her fingertips to her now swollen lips. Her gaze meets mine once again. "Once more. That had to be a fluke."

This time, her fingers grip the collar of my shirt and tug me to her. Her cherry red lips press to mine in a bruising kiss. Firm but delicate at the same time. Much like her personality. Her tongue presses at the seam of my lips and I open for her. Our tongues stroke and caress against each other. She twists her body towards mine, her chair swiveling in the process to get closer to me. I run my hands up her jean covered thighs.

"Hey! None of that shit in my bar. Take it outside." Rusty's deep voice booms from the other end of the bar.

She pulls away slightly. "Outside?"

"Lead the way."

She grabs her purse and hops off the barstool. Earlier I got to admire her front, now I get to appreciate her backside. Her hair cascades to the middle of her back. I'm itching to run my fingers through her locks. To wrap the strands around my hand and tug, show her exactly where I want her uppity mouth. When we reach the exit, she pushes the metal bar on the door, and I hold it open as we both step out into the humid summer evening. I continue to follow her as she rounds the corner to the side of the building. Mostly, I'm curious how far she wants to take this. Either way, I'm ready for whatever she wants.

Once we're in the building's shadow from the setting sun, she rests her back against the wall. In one swift motion, she grabs my wrist and tugs so my body is flush with hers. My palm presses against the wall, creating a barrier between us and the street. The rough brick is a stark contrast against my palm compared to her soft skin.

13

Her tongue peeks out. My gaze lingers as she slowly swipes from one corner of her mouth to the other.

"Are you waiting for a formal invitation in the mail to kiss me again, or what?" Her piercing blue eyes shine bright, even in the darkest shadows as they meet mine.

"I'm gonna have to do something with that smart mouth of yours."

"What are you waiting for? You're certainly doing a lot of talking for a bad boy who says he doesn't ask but takes." She lifts her chin in defiance.

*What the hell did I get myself into?*

I grip her chin and slam my lips to hers.

This kiss is even hotter than in the bar. Maybe because we're a little more secluded, but whatever the reason, I'm here for it. Again, she takes charge and presses her tongue to my seam and I open. Our tongues swirl and caress each other's, the kiss growing hotter with each passing second. The bulge in my pants presses against her belly and she moans. Her grip on my waist tightens as she draws me closer. We are so close, you couldn't slip a sheet of paper between us.

Laughter from a group of people echoes between the buildings, growing louder as they draw near. I pull away but keep my mouth inches from hers.

Her eyes flutter open. "That was ... I don't … I'm …"

"Speechless? Because I didn't think that was possible."

"Something like that." Her words are barely a whisper.

At that moment, my phone buzzes. I retreat, pulling it from my pocket, and read the text message.

"I gotta go." And not because I want to. If given a choice, I would much rather stay here and see how the rest of this pans out, but my friend Archie needs me.

"Yeah. I should get going, too." She turns to move, then pauses. "Thanks for being my test subject." Her fingers press to her lips, then she whirls around and strolls out of the alley onto the sidewalk.

Her hair flutters in the light breeze. My hand twitches with the temptation to go after her, drag her to my place, and finish what we started. I shake the thought from my head. Instead, I turn and leave the alley in the opposite direction. Leaving everything that just happened behind me.

# CHAPTER THREE

## KISSING BETS

*Olivia*

All weekend I thought about the kiss, dreamed about the kiss, and fantasized about the kiss. Except in the last one, we didn't stop at just the kiss. I rest my elbow on my desk and drop my chin onto my open palm. I huff out a sigh as a strand of hair flutters in front of my face before falling back into place. Monday mornings used to be fun when I worked the front desk next to my best friend, Charlie. But after she started dating Bennett, they both left The Blue Stone Group, the largest real estate and development group in the region. Our other friend Parisa's still here, but she's so busy running the marketing department I rarely get to see her during the day.

Trey strolls through the front door in his pristinely tailored, navy Brooks Brothers pinstriped suit and tobacco-colored loafers. When he comes in here with his hot, take charge, business man persona, I wish our kiss sent tingles to my vagina. But no, apparently that only happens with gruff, grumpy bad boys who I'm sure don't even own a suit. But hell, he would be a tasty treat in one. An image of him pops into my mind, but then dissipates as quickly as it appears. Frustrated, I blow out another huff.

A shadow casts over the papers in front of me. When I glance up, Trey's bright smile is shining down on me. Trey's one of the head realtors at The Blue Stone Group. He took over when Bennett left.

"Is that depressed look because our kiss didn't work out? Because if you want, we can go down to the T.W.A.T. closet and try again." He rests an elbow on the two-tier desktop and leans over. The T.W.A.T closet was a storage room in the basement of The Blue Stone Group Trey and his friends turned into a secret hook up spot while at work.

"I thought you dismantled The Weekday Adult Time closet after Bennett left?"

"Well, yeah, but I could always open it back up." He tosses me a wink.

"Thanks for the offer. But that's not it."

"Then what has you looking like someone kicked your puppy?" He clasps his hands together in front of him.

"Well ..." Do I tell him about the mystery man I kissed who clearly finished the job he couldn't? That might be a little harsh. Plus, we were never the kiss and tell kind of friends. Maybe it's best if I keep this little bit of information to myself for now. "It's just ... cramping. That time of the month." I motion my hand around my stomach.

Trey rises to his full height and, not so discreetly, checks his watch. "Look at the time. I have ... a meeting to get ready for. I'll catch you later."

With that, he scurries away to the bank of elevators along the far wall of the atrium. Once he's out of sight, I sigh. Again. What I wouldn't do to see the hot, bad boy again. We could finish what we started and this time, end the night between the sheets. When he called me duchess … something about that pet name sent my heart careening into the atmosphere. It wasn't like he was calling me sweetheart or baby. I would have smacked him for that. A smile plays on my lips. *Duchess.*

My cell phone buzzes in my purse, startling me. I pull open the desk drawer and rifle through everything to get to it. Glancing down, *Mom* flashes on the screen, even though she knows I'm at work. If I don't answer her call, she'll just keep calling. I press the green button.

"Hi Mom."

"Remember, tomorrow we have a meeting with the caterers to discuss the menu for the charity gala." No warm greeting. Not a hi or how are you, just right to business, as if she forgot she's talking to her daughter.

"Yes, Mom. It's on my calendar," I lie. It's not on my calendar.

"Okay. I wanted to make sure it wouldn't be like last time."

"I got a flat tire. It's not like I slashed my own tire so I didn't have to go." That was my second option, but luckily a nail did the job for me. And she never lets me forget it.

"Don't be so crass."

"Okay, Mom. But I have to get going. I'm working. I'll see you then."

"Be sure to wear something nice. Not one of those low-cut shirts you like to wear. Why buy the cow—"

I roll my eyes. "Cow. Milk. Got it. I'll be sure to wear a turtleneck." Even though it's eighty degrees outside.

"Maybe a nice blouse like the Veronica Beard puff-sleeve top. Just be sure to button all the—"

"Okay, Mom."

"I wish you would find a nice man like your sister. Someone who's made a name for himself."

What she really means is a guy who has money. Who's more than likely sleeping with an intern or assistant. Much like my father. Hard pass.

"Doctor Jones has a newly single son—"

"I gotta get back to work. See you later. Okay. Byeee."

I pull my phone away while she's mid-sentence and press end. She's exhausting on the best of days. Don't get me wrong, I love my mom, but she takes her job as a socialite way too seriously. If she isn't organizing some charity gala, she's arranging a formal brunch, or she's planning some lavish trip, which may or may not include my father. Planning the parties is my favorite part, even if I have to deal with my mom. At least my younger sister, Tatum, is always at my side and takes some of the pressure off me and my lackluster love life. If I have to hear, "Olivia, how can a beautiful woman like you still be single? When are you going to settle down?" And my favorite. "You're not getting any younger. Everything won't stay perky forever." I'm going to end up in an orange jumpsuit. Thirty-one is not old. Everything is still perky, thank you very much. I square my shoulders and glance down. The girls look exceptional today in this blouse. They are definitely not lacking in the perky department.

"Admiring your boobs again?" Parisa drops her bag from her shoulder and it hits the ground with a thud. I glance up with my chest still puffed out. "They look fantastic today. New bra?"

"No. Just gravity not taking its toll on them yet." My shoulders fall. "So, what's up? How was your weekend?"

"Exhausting. Taking care of a one-year-old, is draining. Then Seth is continuously trying to sex me up, hoping to have another baby. Which is sweet he wants another child, but also draining. Sadly, I'm excited to be at work so I can have five minutes to myself."

Parisa met her boyfriend and now baby daddy while they both worked here at The Blue Stone Group in the marketing department. One day they hated each other. The hatred grew more and more every day. Eventually, it became as big as a hot air balloon ready to burst which didn't help when a promotion pinned them against each other. After a work trip to Colorado left them stranded together, the balloon burst. The hatred turned to passion, and they worked out their differences between the sheets.

"That must be *so* cumbersome to have your nerdy, sexy boyfriend tie you up with his bow ties and have his wicked way with you." I dramatically roll my eyes.

"Don't get me wrong, I love every minute of it. But sometimes I want to be the one to tie him up, and leave him there, just so I can have a few minutes to myself." Parisa huffs as she throws her weight against the desk. She props her head up on her hand. "Anyway, how was your weekend?"

Do I tell her everything that happened? The longer time goes on, it feels more and more like a lucid dream. "I kissed a guy."

Parisa claps her hands in front of her and squeals. "Please tell me you put all of us out of our misery and you've finally hooked up with Trey." She taps her chin. "In fact, I believe I picked July on the board."

"Um. What board?"

She digs out her phone and taps on the screen a few times. "Shit. That was Charlie. Lucky bitch," she mutters.

"Hello? What are you talking about?"

"Oh. We kinda started a board with months that you and Trey would finally get together." She tucks her phone into her bag.

"Hold on. You guys placed bets on when Trey and I would hook up?"

"Well ... yeah. I guess. You two have been pulling at each other's attraction cords for so long. It was only a matter of time before it finally happened. We decided to have a bit of fun with it."

A part of me is hurt and a little betrayed that my friends gambled on my love life. But also, I wish I could have gotten in on that. "How much was the pot?"

She taps her chin thinking. "Since it went on for so long, it might be up to one thousand dollars."

My jaw drops as my eyes go wide. "A thousand dollars. Why didn't I know about this?"

"Because that would be cheating. Anyway, who'd you kiss?" She leans in closer, eagerness in her eyes, wanting all the juicy details.

"Well, technically, it was two guys." I hold up two fingers.

Her eyes go wide. "In the same night?"

I nod.

"You hussy. So, spill it already."

"Trey was the first guy."

"Ahh! I knew it! Tell me everything." She rubs her hands together, expecting to get the dirty details. Unfortunately, the only dirty details were stuck to the bottom of my shoe.

"Honestly, there isn't much to tell." I shrug.

Parisa tilts her head to the side. "What do you mean?"

"Have you ever built something up inside your head, like you've hyped it up so much you're just waiting for it to

21

explode with amazingness? But instead, all you get is a party popper filled with confetti that doesn't unravel."

"I've read a few books like that ..." She shrugs one shoulder.

"It was like that. We kissed and I was expecting to be engulfed in a burning pit of heat and passion, but instead it was like a dud bottle rocket. We lit the wick, but never shot off."

"Oh shit. Like he couldn't ..." She holds her pointer finger down then straight, repeating the motion. "That ... sucks. With all the flirting, I was expecting something."

"We didn't even get to that! All we did was kiss, but it was so ... disappointing. Maybe we are just better off as friends."

"So that's one guy. Who's the second?"

Heat creeps up my neck reminiscing about him and our kiss. "So, Trey left The Blue Anchor—"

"This all happened at The Blue Anchor?"

"It was Trey's idea. He figured it would be one place where no one would recognize us. Anyway, after Trey left, I sat at the bar to have a drink and figure out what the hell had just happened. I had convinced myself I was broken. There is no reasonable explanation why I wouldn't have felt anything when I kissed Trey. Next to me, there was a guy. He was attractive in a rough-around-the-edges kind of way, so I told him to kiss me."

She perks up as she leans in. "And what happened?"

I flop backward, my back hitting the chair. "It was a kiss that trumps all kisses. The instant our lips touched, everything inside me exploded with a fury of heat and passion. A burning hot desire for this stranger at the bar."

"What happened next?" Parisa's phone buzzes in her bag and she picks it up. "Hold that thought." She steps away from the desk to take the phone call. A few seconds later, she turns toward me. "Emergency meeting upstairs. Call the girls. Porter's tonight. I need to know what happened next." She wiggles her fingers in a wave and then she's briskly walking toward the bank of elevators.

Once again, I'm left dreaming about the kiss with the mystery guy.

Later that evening Parisa, Charlie, Hollyn, Tatum, and I are all gathered around our usual table at Porter's Ale House. It's our home away from home, and our general meeting spot for girls nights. Plus Jake, the owner, gives us free drinks and you never turn down a free drink. I give the girls the same rundown I gave Parisa earlier. Everything that happened with Trey and when I get to the point of the story about locking lips with the sexy bad boy, my thighs clench together.

"It was a feeling I've never felt before. I was a half a second away from telling him to come home with me, but then he got a message and had to leave." I pout.

"Did you get his number?" Charlie asks.

My teeth sink into my lower lip as I shake my head.

"You at least got his name, right?" Hollyn asks.

I flinch slightly and shake my head again.

Parisa bends her neck forward as her voice goes quiet. "Wait, so you know what the inside of his mouth feels like, but you don't know his name?"

I groan. "I know. It's so unlike me. We were in the throes of this amazing kiss. I wasn't thinking straight. My focus was on the way his lips moved against mine. The way his hands clung to my waist. The slight bite to his grip. Not painful, but in an 'I want you right now' kind of way."

"Oh yes. Like he might leave little fingerprint bruises on you. Bennett's done that a few times. It's hot." Charlie nods.

"Yes. Exactly that. Just without Bennett." I smirk. "But

23

then his buzzing phone interrupted our make-out session. From there he left, and I was left wanton." My gaze drops to my half empty margarita in front of me.

"I'm still in disbelief that you let him go. Not like you." Tatum reaches for her glass and takes a sip.

"I know. I blame it on the lust induced haze I was in. No way could I think straight after what he did. But I don't know what to do now. Replaying our kiss while using my best vibrator only lasts for so long before I forget what it was actually like," I whine. I've spent many nights, more times than I like to admit, with a vibrator. In fact, that reminds me I need to buy more batteries. While I do have a rechargeable vibrator, nothing is worse than chasing the big O and your vibrator dies. It's like having sex and the guy falls asleep mid stroke. Or stopping to charge leads to a lackluster climax. Or swapping vibes, which has you imagining you're in your very own real life why choose romance with the different sizes, shapes, and textures. At least with batteries you swap them out relatively fast and keep going instead of trying to enjoy yourself with a corpse of a vibrator.

"Then we find him." Charlie slams her fist on the table and our drinks rattle.

"How? Wander the streets asking everyone if they've seen a hot bad boy?" This idea has crossed my mind a time or two. I just never worked up to actually doing it.

"You could get a character sketch drawn and hang up a poster. Wanted. This hot and sexy bad boy is wanted for a night of passionate, animalistic sex." Tatum throws her head back as if she's the one being ravished right now. An eruption of laughter comes from our table.

"No!" Parisa throws up her hands, palms out. "I got it! We know he goes to The Blue Anchor. Maybe he's a frequent customer?"

"Another stake out! But maybe this time without the bushes," Charlie says.

When Charlie found out her now ex-boyfriend was cheating on her, we came up with a plan to catch him in the act which involved spying on him through a restaurant window which led us to being accosted by some touchy feely bushes.

"Oh yes! That's way better than my idea," Tatum says with a laugh.

"So, I just need to go hang out at The Blue Anchor and hope he shows up again?" I glance down at my black, knee-length skirt and metallic sheen top. "Because I won't stick out like a sore thumb."

"How else do you expect to find him? This is the only lead we have," Charlie says.

"Okay. I'll just go to The Blue Anchor and hope I see him again. But what if I do see him? What do I say?" My mind races. I don't know what I would do if I saw him again. Probably tell him to kiss me.

"Holy shit. You must really like this guy. You've never been this frazzled over someone before." Parisa sets down her drink.

I've dated many guys over the years, but none of them have implanted themselves in me as fast and as hard as the bad boy has. "I guess for as much as I can like a guy without knowing his name. So, I'm doing this. I'm going to find the hot bad boy." I just hope I'm not disappointed if I see him again.

# CHAPTER FOUR

# TROUBLE'S A BREWING

## Ledger

I crank the wrench, but the bolt holding the mount doesn't budge. All morning I've been working on rebuilding the engine of a two-thousand-three Harley Davidson Sportster. Currently, the carburetor and its mount are being a real bitch. With one last turn, the bolt breaks free. One down, one more to go. But even this rebuild can't distract me from the blonde duchess from The Blue Anchor. She's infiltrated my dreams every night since we met. I'm kicking myself for not getting her number because I wouldn't mind pushing her against a wall again. When I saw the text message, all my thoughts went somewhere else. My focus was only on one thing, and it was no longer her.

The rumble of a motorcycle engine pulling into the parking lot of my shop draws my attention from the second bolt. A familiar bike comes into view, and I rise to my feet.

I set the wrench on the tool bench and grab a blue shop rag, wiping the grease and oil from my hands before tossing it onto the bench.

Archie, a longtime friend, comes to a halt just outside the large overhead garage door, kicks down the kickstand, and swings his leg over his bike. When I'm standing in front of him, I hold out my hand for a shake. He grips it and pulls me in for a one handed back pat.

"Long time no see. I thought you retired this one years ago." I glance down and admire the black 1953 Indian Chief. With its sleek lines and streamlined skirted fenders, it's a beauty.

"After spending countless hours fixing it up, I was tired of watching it collect dust. You remember those long, grueling hours. It was great having you right by my side in my garage."

A weak smile plays on my lips. "Yes, I remember those nights. And how much Stevie hated them."

"That's because she wanted to spend her time with you, but you wanted to spend your time working on engines."

I give him a tight smile because he's not wrong. At the time, I was more interested in taking engines apart and rebuilding them than playing house. Every free hour I had, I was in the garage with Archie. I suspected she was jealous of how much time I was spending on the bike instead of chasing her. Eventually, she wore me down but could never get over the fact my first love would always be a wrench. "Why the visit? Heard anything from Stevie?"

The night at The Blue Anchor, Archie's text was asking if I'd seen or heard from his daughter. While our relationship has been over for years, I don't want anything to happen to her because I know Archie would be devastated.

He purses his lips and shakes his head. The wrinkles around his eyes have grown more prominent over the years. I'm sure Stevie is the cause of more than a few of them.

"After all these years, I still can't believe she's doing this shit."

"Well, you're familiar with her free spirit and how she'll take off for days at a time—"

"Part of the reason it never worked out between us." I cross my arms over my chest.

"Yeah. Unfortunately, it's been more than a few days this time."

"How long?"

"A week."

"Damn." I shake my head. "And you haven't heard anything. No text? No phone call?"

"Nothing. While this isn't unlike her, I wish she would let me know she's alright. I've made a few phone calls to some people she typically sees when she's gone, but they haven't heard from her either." Silence fills the space between us. "Too bad you two couldn't make it work. You would have been one hell of a son-in-law. You might have even kept her grounded."

Archie has been like a father to me since I was a seventeen-year-old punk running the streets. He took me in and kicked my ass into shape. After I got my shit together, he gave me a job working in his shop. Then I met his daughter. She was always parading herself around the garage, but she had no interest in tools. For years, it was great. I thought we would marry and become the family I never had. But that was the biggest lie I ever told myself.

I shake my head. "A man can only take so much before

he cuts ties and becomes numb." My gaze falls to the cement floor.

"Maybe she'll get her shit together and you two can try again. You were the only person she really listened to."

No way that's going to happen. She had multiple chances, and she fucked up every single one of them. "She liked the thrill of the chase but got bored once she got what she wanted."

"She was always a wild one." He pauses. "If you hear from her or she stops by, let me know."

"Of course. Anything for you." What I really want to tell him is that she's an adult and is making her own decisions. He can't be there to bail her out whenever she gets in trouble. But he'll do anything for his daughter, and I'll do anything for him. So, if he wants me to be on the lookout, that's what I'll do.

He clasps my shoulder, the hard lines on his face soften. He's a man who's been through a lot, especially when it comes to his daughter, but he'll always have a soft heart for her, regardless of what kind of trouble she's found.

"Take care, Ledger." He gets on his bike and starts it up. I stand in the opening of the overhead garage door as he's exiting the parking lot, the rumble of his engine growing quieter the farther away he gets.

I've owned my shop for over seven years and it's all thanks to Archie. Not only did he teach me everything I know, but he also fronted me the money to buy it. It's nothing over the top or fancy with the latest and greatest equipment, but it's modest with four bays with two lifts. And it gets the job done. Over the years, my customer base grew, and I was able to repay him in under five years. Then I hired my friend Jay. Since then, I've hired a few part time mechanics, mostly to give myself a day off.

"Archie hasn't been around for a while. What did he

want?" Jay stands next to me, arms crossed. When I don't answer him right away, he continues, "Do you smell that?"

I glance his way and he's sniffing the air. I glare at him but say nothing.

"Smells like trouble is a brewing on the horizon." He wiggles his eyebrows.

I shove his shoulder. "Get back to work. I'm not paying you to gossip."

"For you, that's free." He points a finger at me with his signature cocky smile.

I pivot and brush past him on my way to the workbench. I'd walk through fire for Archie. Without his help, I wouldn't be where I am right now. And my heart wouldn't be chained and locked without Stevie. My palms rest against the edge of the tool bench and I bow my head. I don't have time to ponder this. She's already occupied too many of my thoughts. I exhale a deep breath and push off. When I turn, Jay startles me as he stands next to me. "Jesus Christ. Now, this is just getting creepy. You're like that guy in *Mr. Deeds*. You just pop up out of nowhere."

"The last time I saw you like this a certain raven-haired beauty came back to town." He cocks an eyebrow.

"Good job CSI. Maybe you should quit your mechanic job."

"And leave you to your own devices … never. So, I'm right, aren't I?"

"She does what she always does. Now we all just wait and see if and when she shows up."

He hums the *Jeopardy* theme song with a smug smile on his face. I narrow my gaze in his direction before shouldering past him. I don't have time for this shit. My feet pound on the cement as I make my way to the other side of the garage and down a narrow hallway. Once I reach my office, I kick the door shut with my heel. I swivel my desk chair around then throw myself down. It's always the same shit different day with Stevie. Even when she's not physically here, she still manages to send my life into a tailspin. This isn't about her anymore. I've been over her for years, but I owe it to Archie. Hell, I owe my life, and this garage, to Archie. I'll do anything for him. I scrub my hands down my face. Fuck. I'm going to be on edge for as long as she's missing.

# CHAPTER FIVE

# TAKE TWO

*Olivia*

All week, I've been on edge. This is completely out of character for me. I'm not the one who pursues the guy. I bring the glass up to my lips and tip it back. The cold light beer hits my lips and I swallow down a gulp. It would be better if this could be anything but beer. I'm contemplating straight vodka at this point. Or anything else to calm my erratic heartbeat. My foot bounces a mile a minute on the bar stool footrest. I found a seat in the corner of the bar to the right of the door, so I have a clear view of anyone entering. Although it wasn't very hard to find a table since there are only a handful of people here. Every time the door opens, I can't help but glance up at the sunlight that enters the dimly lit bar. So far, that door has opened ten times and each time I'm disappointed.

Checking the clock on my phone, I noticed I'm running out of time.

I took everyone's advice to wait at The Blue Anchor hoping for him to show up. I've been here for thirty minutes and nothing. This is dumb. Why am I even here? It was one kiss. Surely, he can't be the only guy in the entire world who sets my body ablaze when his lips touch mine. Instinctively, my fingertips press against my lips. He doesn't have magical lips. Ones that cause my thighs to clench together and my nipples to pebble. Who am I kidding? He does all those things. I sigh. But what if I've hyped up our kiss so much that if I get a second chance, it won't live up to the first?

*Don't get ahead of yourself. You still need the second kiss.*

By the eleventh time the door opens, but who's counting, and my sexy, bad boy doesn't walk in, I give up. He's not going to show. The longer I wait, the more frustrated I become. I pick up my glass and swirl the golden liquid before setting the glass down on the table deciding against the last sip of now warm beer. Rising to my feet, I toss my handbag strap over my shoulder and push in my stool.

I'm a few steps from the exit when the door opens. I glance up, and my heart stops as I come to a halt. In front of me stands a familiar chiseled jaw, dark steely eyes, and silky dark hair. I nervously scan the man in front of me, my breath held tight in my chest. Maybe if I don't move, he won't see me.

"Olivia? What are you doing here?" Trey side steps out of the doorway as another person enters the bar.

"Oh. Um. I came here … for a beer." I clutch my bag closer to me as I shift back and forth in my four-inch heels.

"This place isn't exactly known for their world class beer selection." Trey quirks an eyebrow.

"Well, they have … cold beer." I inwardly cringe.

*Really, cold beer? That's the best I could come up with?*

"I suppose their beer is exceptionally cold. But The Blue Anchor doesn't seem like your type of hang out. Why not hang out at Porter's? I'm sure they have cold beer, too."

I need to get Trey off my back so I can get out of here because if the hot bad boy shows up right now, it could get awkward. Mostly for me, but awkward, nonetheless. "I could ask you the same thing."

"I'm meeting Bennett. We occasionally come here for some peace and quiet with our beer."

"Wait." I dramatically gasp, my fingers covering my mouth. Then I lean in and whisper, "Are you cheating on Porter's with The Blue Anchor?"

Trey's eyes go wide and his body tenses. "Shit. Do you think Jake knows? He has been a little standoffish toward me." Trey glances over his shoulder. "Jake would be so mad. I bet he has spies watching me." He glances over his other shoulder before stopping his gaze on me. "You never saw me here." Pulling his phone out of his pocket and taping the screen. After a few silent moments, he says into the speaker, "Abort mission. I repeat abort mission. Jake has spies at The Blue Anchor. We need to go elsewhere." Slowly, he inches backward, phone still to his ear until he reaches the exit. Then he spins around and throws open the door and rushes out.

As soon as the door closes behind him, my shoulders drop.

*That was close.*

I need to get out of here in case he returns, or worse, I actually run into the hot bad boy. I'm too flustered to see him. Rushing out of the bar, I dash down the sidewalk to where my car that's parked around the corner. I peer down into my bag and rifle through, searching for my phone.

*Oomph*

Suddenly, I'm stumbling backward until an arm wraps around my waist, preventing me from falling on my ass.

"Duchess?" His deep, gruff voice sends a shiver through my body and parks itself right between my legs.

Glancing up, I'm greeted with the same lips that filled my dreams for the past week. My breath hitches. "Oh. Uh. Um."

I've never been one to get tongue tied when talking to guys, but this one makes me forget how to form proper words. Hell, I don't even know if I know my own name right now. Oh. That's all I could come up with. Oh—oh, I could actually use a big one of those right now. Preferably with this guy hovering above me. I snap myself out of my daydream and fumble to steady myself on my feet.

"There you are. I was getting concerned. Your eyes glazed over and—"

"Uh yeah. No. I'm good." Real good. My body burns where his hand is still gripping my waist. Get yourself together. I scold myself. You've spent the last hour hoping to see him and now he's standing in front of you and all you can spew are half sentences. I shake my head. "Kiss me," I whisper.

He tilts his head as his lips tip up into a half smile.

I inwardly cringe. Guess I'm two for two. "Oh, God." I smack my forehead. "It was the first thing that came to mind. Then I just word vomited all over you." I drag my hand down his black t-shirt, and over his chiseled chest, to wipe away the word vomit. "That's nice." I purr as I continue petting his chest. A deep rumble sounds from his chest, breaking me from my lust filled trance. I drop my hand to my side. "Sorry. I was hoping to run into you again. That's why I'm here. I haven't stopped thinking about our first kiss and I really wanted another one and now I'm rambling. I never ramble but—"

He brings his hand up and clasps his fingers around the nape of my neck and hauls me to him. My eyebrows shoot up to my hairline, but of course, I go willingly. This is the second time he's handled me like this. Not sweet and caring like every other guy has done, but it's possessive and wild. A spark ignites and courses through my entire body just from his touch. Then his lips are on mine. Demanding and harsh, and hot as hell. It's everything I remembered and more. I snake one hand up his stomach and grip the front of his well-worn t-shirt, needing to hold on to something so I don't float away. Needing more of him, I press closer into his body and deepen the kiss. Our tongues caress and stroke against each other's. His grip on my neck tightens and I half groan from the pain and moan from the pleasure. With his body pressed up against mine, he can do whatever he wants to me.

I pull from the kiss, my breathing labored. "That was better than the first time."

"I'll promise to make the third and fourth even better."

An eruption of butterflies take flight inside me. He wants more. "My name is Olivia Ellis." My words are soft and breathy.

"Ledger Hudson."

His name even sounds bad boyish. I imagine how it would sound rolling off my tongue as he brings me to orgasm. And I really want to test it out. My phone buzzes in my purse, and I know it's my mom wondering where I am for our charity meeting. I inwardly roll my eyes. Even when she's not here, she still manages to ruin everything.

I sigh. "I have to get going."

"Is this payback for kissing and leaving last time?" The

corner of his lips pull into a smile, a small dimple forms on his left cheek.

I chuckle. "I have a meeting I need to get to before I'm late."

He nods. "So, can I have your number or should we just plan to run into each other again at The Blue Anchor?"

"As much as I love our meetings, phone numbers sound like a better idea." I dig for my phone in my purse, unlock it, and pass it to him. "Add your number." Once he types in his number, he passes my phone back to me. I glance down at the screen name he gave himself. "Sexy Bad Boy, huh?"

"I didn't want you to forget."

*Like I could forget him.*

I type out a message to him and hit send, so he has my number as well. When his phone buzzes, he pulls it out from his front pocket, saving my number, and shoving it back into his jeans.

"I won't keep you from your meeting. I hope to hear from you soon, duchess."

Why do I turn into mush when he calls me that? Normally, I hate pet names, but his deep voice has a certain way of making this one sound so sexy.

We both head in different directions. He continues on his way toward the bar and I find my car. The temptation to blow off this meeting and follow him to find out how this day could end is strong. Faking a flat is sounding pretty good right now.

## CHAPTER SIX

# MIC DROP MOMENT

*Olivia*

I pick up the phone, then set it down, repeating this five more times. It's been three days, why hasn't Ledger called me or texted me? It could be as simple as "hey, it was great seeing you again" or "hey, want to make out again." I'm game for either one.

After work, I called an emergency meeting at Porter's. I take a seat at our usual table under a neon brewery sign that hangs on the weathered wood plank wall. Porter's has a dive bar charm but with a splash of industrial aesthetic with exposed ductwork. Also, the barn wood and sheet metal décor give it rustic vibe.

I need my girls to talk me off the Ledger ledge I've found myself desperately perched on. Gripping my margarita glass, I swallow down the last of its contents. As I set my empty glass down, Tatum and Hollyn stroll through the door and spot me immediately.

"Charlie's busy helping Bennett with a custom table build so she won't be coming," Tatum says as she takes a seat next to me.

"And Parisa's helping Seth at the Lilith House, so she won't make it either," Hollyn says, sitting down across from us.

"Okay, I need your advice. Ledger. After running into him again and exchanging numbers, I haven't heard back. What do I do?" I've run every possible scenario as to why I haven't heard from him, starting with he lost his phone, which means he lost my number, to he has a girlfriend and I'm actually the other woman who helped him cheat. While I'd like to believe it's the first one, the longer I don't hear from him, the more I'm convinced it's the latter.

"First, we need a round of drinks before we tackle this." Tatum jumps from her seat and saunters up to the bar. She returns with three margaritas in her hands.

Over the next hour, and another round later, we chat about Tatum's hot lawyer boyfriend, Adam, and how he's booked a Caribbean vacation for them this fall. Hollyn tells us about the new cupcakes she's been working on, along with the new dance moves Van has been learning. He's currently practicing the cowboy hip thrust, and it's everything the move is named for. Hollyn's words, not mine. When the conversation shifts to me, my face is already flush. I don't know if it's from the margaritas or talking about Ledger, but I lift my hair off my neck. The cool air is refreshing, then I let my locks fall.

"So, you haven't heard from this guy yet?" Tatum takes a sip of her drink.

"It's been three days and I've heard nothing from Ledger. Why hasn't he called? Do you think he's changed his mind?" I glance between Hollyn and Tatum, praying one of them has an answer. I need answers.

"You must really like this guy. Normally, you're a full-on take charge woman, but he's turned you into a bumbling, hot mess," Tatum says.

"Ledger has me in uncharted territory. First of all, he's the complete opposite of any guy I've been with. He's not clean cut, doesn't have perfectly styled hair, and doesn't wear a suit. I don't know what to do." My throat constricts. I'm at a loss. I've never had a guy propel me into such a tailspin before, and I don't know if I'll be able to correct myself. Or if I'll just crash into the ground. Everyone I've dated has been either a doctor, lawyer, CEO, or the son of one of those. Someone always introduced me to one of them, and I never had to make the first phone call.

"You took charge when you kissed him. Just do that again." Hollyn takes a sip of her drink. "I think we're old enough to be past this whole, waiting to call someone one we like because we don't want to appear desperate." She throws up air quotes at the word desperate.

I gasp. "I never said I was desperate."

"You're right. You're not desperate, but you need to go after what you want." Hollyn squares her shoulders.

"She's not wrong," Tatum says. "Games get you nowhere. You'll just end up driving yourself crazy. And all your friends." She nudges me with her elbow.

"So, I should call him?" I glance between my two friends.

"Yes! Take charge!" Hollyn holds her drink in the air.

"Put your big girl panties on and show him exactly who Olivia Gretchen Ellis is. Strong. Fierce. And doesn't need to wait for a guy to call her." Tatum lifts her glass to meet Hollyn's.

"And if he doesn't respond, to hell with him. You'll find someone better," Hollyn says.

"I'm going to call him!" I straighten myself in my chair and raise my glass to join theirs above the middle of our table.

"Girl, you go call the hell out of him," Tatum encourages.

"I'm going to take charge. I don't need him to call me because I'm going to call him." I don't know if it's the encouragement from my friends or the tequila flowing through my veins, but I'm doing this. We clink our glasses together and we all take a drink. Mine may have been a little bigger, or a lot bigger, then theirs. But I'm the one putting it all out there. Digging into my purse, I pull out my phone and hover my finger over his number. My heart races in my chest and my cheeks flush. What am I going to say when he answers? What if he doesn't answer? Do I leave a message? Hang up? A hand appears on top of mine, pressing my finger to the screen. *Sexy Bad Boy* pops up on the screen and a timer starts. I shoot a glare at Tatum.

She shrugs. "You were taking too long."

My fingers shake as I fumble with my phone. It almost crashes to the table but I'm able to get a grip and bring it to my ear. The line rings. And rings. My heartbeat thumps in my throat as I tap at the base of my margarita glass with my nail needing something to do as I anxiously wait for him to answer. It rings again, then his voicemail picks up. I have approximately five seconds to decide what to do next. Hang up or leave a message. The voicemail beeps, and I can't hang up now, so I opt for a long, detailed message.

Once I'm done, I jab my finger on the end button, which isn't as satisfying as slamming the receiver down with a corded telephone, but it's done. The next move is his.

"We need another drink." I mic drop my phone into my purse.

# CHAPTER SEVEN

# NO HOLDING HANDS

*Ledger*

As I turn the faucet of my shower off, I hear the tail end of my phone ringing. I pull open the curtain and Jack meows at me before jumping off the bathroom counter. Yanking the towel off the bar, I run it down my face before wrapping it around my waist, securing it in front. I follow Jack out to the living room. He jumps up on the couch and I take a seat next to him. I grab my phone off the coffee table. Unlocking the screen, a *Missed Call Duchess* message pops up. My lips tug into a smile. This week has been hell. Every available second, I itched to call her, but something always came up and distracted me. She was done waiting and decided to take matters into her own hands. And hell if that doesn't turn me on. The voicemail icon catches my attention. I press it and turn on the speakerphone. There's a moment of silence before her sweet voice fills the room.

*It's been three days, and you never called me, so I'm tugging on my big girl panties and calling you.*

Her words slur a little at the end as noise fills the background. She's out somewhere, and she's been drinking.

*You don't get to ghost me. If you want to kiss me and never talk to me again, you need to tell me to my face. I'm right here, come tell me. If you lost your phone and you never get this message, that really sucks. And if the real reason you never called is because you're married with ten kids, well fu—*

The message cuts off. I stifle a laugh, imagining what the last few words of that sentence were. I check the time on my phone. 9 p.m. It's not too late. I pull up her number and press call. After a few rings, she picks up. I can hear muted noises of people talking and music playing in the background, so I know she's still at the bar.

"Oh, look who decides to call now."

I want to kiss that sass from her mouth. "Where are you?"

"Wouldn't you like to know where I am?"

"That's why I asked. You want me to tell you to your face, so tell me, where are you?"

"Porter's! We're at Porters!" someone yells in the background. Then I hear Olivia, but she isn't talking to me. "What the hell, Tatum? That's not how big girl panties work …"

I hang up, jump to my feet, and dash into my bedroom. Tossing on whatever clean clothes I can find, I snatch my truck keys from the kitchen and bolt out the door. Ten minutes later, I'm pulling into the parking lot of Porter's Ale House. For a weekday, this place is busy. Luckily, I find a parking spot close to the door just as another vehicle is leaving. Turning off the ignition, I jump out and traverse the parking lot. I open the door and scan the large room. My height gives me an advantage to peer over most of the crowd. Then I spot her, sitting at a far table with two other women. Her beauty making her hard not to notice. I'm surprised her table isn't swarming with guys wanting to talk to her. Good thing there's not, otherwise, I'd have to rip them all away.

I march my way through the crowd. Her sweet laughter fills my ears the closer I get to her table. As I approach, she's seated at the end of the high top table, back toward me. Her two friends take notice first, their jaws dropping and eyes going wide. The one who's an uncanny resemblance to Olivia jabs her with her elbow. She jolts and whirls around. Shock covers her face before she gains her composure.

Her eyes scan mine. "What are you doing here?"

"You told me if I wanted to kiss you and never talk to you again, I had to tell you to your face."

She sits up straight as if she's preparing for a punch. "Well, say it."

"Can we go somewhere private?"

She lifts her chin. "Whatever you have to say, you can say it in front of my friends."

Not how I envisioned doing this, but okay. I step up to her causing her to crane her neck to meet my gaze. Lifting my hand, I grip the nape of her neck over her golden locks and slam my lips to hers. She releases a small squeak in surprise. Her fingers dance up my covered torso, gripping the fabric to keep me close. Her sweet jasmine scent wafts around me. Pulling away, I break the kiss, but I keep my lips centimeters from hers.

"See, I was going to call you, but my week has been shit, including today. Then I got your message, so I figured

45

I needed to clear a few things up. I didn't lose my phone. I'm not married. And have zero kids. Are you happy now?"

Her eyes flutter open. Blue irises with flecks of gold surround her dilated pupils. She parts her cherry red lips but says nothing. Instead, she nods.

"And now I'm going to take you home. Clearly, you've been drinking, and I don't want you driving." She nods again. "Two for two on making you speechless. I never thought that would be possible. Let's go." I release my grip on her neck and drag my fingers down her back, coming to a stop just above the curve of her ass. I turn to her friends. "Hi, I'm Ledger."

"Oh, we know." A woman with long auburn hair holds out her hand to me. "I'm Hollyn."

"And I'm Tatum." She extends her hand to me.

"Tatum's my sister," Olivia says as she lifts her purse to her shoulder.

"Will you ladies be okay to get home?"

"Don't worry about us." She waves me off. "Just make sure to take care of that one," Hollyn says with a wink.

I guide her away from the table and through the crowd. "So, you think you can just come here and take me home?"

"Are you going to stop me?"

Her teeth sink into her bottom lip for a brief second. "Actually, no."

"That's what I thought." When we reach the door, I hold it open as she walks through. The warm summer air hits us. A few lamp posts scattered around the parking lot provide a little light in the dark. "Where's your car?" I ask.

"Wait." She stops in her tracks. "How'd you get here? How are you getting home?"

"I drove and don't worry about it. Now, where's your car?"

I tug her along, but she digs her heels in, not moving an inch. "You're so concerned about me getting home. Why can't I be concerned about you getting home?"

I blow out a breath, my patience wearing razor thin. I've never had a girl be so defiant yet turn me. It makes me want to swat her ass and kiss her at the same time. "I'll call for a ride. Happy? Now, where did you park?"

"What are you going to do about work tomorrow?"

"Jesus Christ. Enough with the damn questions." I bend down and press my shoulder into her stomach, and lift. She screams and squirms as I hold her in place.

"Oh, my god! What are you doing?" Her voice is loud enough anyone in the parking lot could hear her. Thankfully, it's empty. I'd rather not have to explain that I'm not kidnapping her against her will, but it's an approved kidnapping.

"Finding your car." First, I pat her pants pocket, but come up empty handed in the key department. Then I reach around for her purse and yank it from her hand.

"Hey!" The laughter in her voice gives her away. She continues to kick and wiggle, wanting to break free, but I'm stronger.

"This would have been easier if you just did as I said. Then I wouldn't need to resort to carrying you." I awkwardly hold her purse in my hand that's wrapped around her legs while my other digs around, searching for her keys.

"I thought cavemen were extinct."

"Nope. We evolved." My fingers grab hold of a set of keys and I yank it out. I situate her purse in one hand and her keys in the other. "Now we spank bad girls who don't listen."

"You wouldn't dare." She kicks her feet up.

"Keep testing me and you'll see for yourself."

I press the lock button and can hear a faint beeping in the distance. I continue to press it, following the sound until her SUV's flashing lights come into view. When we reach her vehicle, I pull open the passenger door. Standing in the opening, I release her legs and she slides down the front of my body. Once her high-heeled feet hit the pavement, she continues to drag the palms of her hands down until they come to a rest on my chest. Her fingers stroke the worn fabric. The slightest touch from her makes me forget my own name.

"Are you going to sit or am I going to need to do that for you, too?"

Her big doe eyes meet mine, and she nibbles on her bottom lip. "I'd rather sit on something else."

I scrub my hands down my face and groan. I lock eyes with her. "Get in the car." I'm about ten seconds away from pushing her against the side of her car and kissing the hell out of her and her smart mouth. Then I'd put that mouth to work on other things. But she saves herself from moaning my name in public when she climbs in. I slam the door and round the hood. Opening the driver's door, I immediately move the seat back, otherwise my knees would be in my chest and my balls would be in my throat. I get in and press the button to start it. Based on her fancy clothes, I shouldn't be surprised she drives an Audi Q8.

I pop it into drive and roll through the parking lot. "What's your address?"

"725 Chestnut Street."

I blow out a low whistle.

"What's that for?" Her tone is defensive.

"That's on the other side of town …"

"And? What? That too far for you?"

"No, it's just that …" I pause, wanting to find the right words without sounding like an asshole. "In that neighborhood, people drive cars more expensive than my house."

She laughs. "Sure, it's a nice area and I'm sure there are some people who may be like that." She shrugs. "My parents wanted me somewhere safe."

"Your parents? As in you still live with them or they live with you?"

"No. They paid for my house, so they made sure it was a safe neighborhood."

I want to tell her being with me isn't somewhere safe. But she'll learn that soon enough. She's prim and proper and I'm all hard edges. She drives expensive cars, and I'm just the man who fixes them. But I'm finding it hard to resist the magnetic pull I have toward her.

Twenty minutes later, I'm pulling into her driveway. A light by the front door illuminates a small wraparound porch. Even though her house is smaller compared to some of her neighbors, mine is still only half the size. She opens her door and jumps out. I quickly follow, wanting to be somewhat of a gentleman, and walk her to the front door. When we're under the soft porch light, I pass her the car keys.

Her smile is wide as her gaze meets mine. "I'm glad I called you tonight. Because who knows if you were ever going to actually call me?"

I bark out a laugh. "If I did, we would have never gotten tonight."

"God forbid we didn't have drunken voicemails and bad boys who whisk you away." She flings her arm in front of her.

I take a step closer and bend down so my lips are inches from hers. "And a sexy as hell duchess with a mouth I want to put to work."

Her breath hitches. "Is that so?"

"Yep." I close the distance and press my lips to hers. Her kiss does something to me. Something unlike anything I've ever felt. I could spend hours kissing this girl. Her little moans and whimpers grow louder as she presses her body against mine. I wrap an arm around her waist to keep her tight to me, wanting to devour every inch of her.

A horn from a passing car breaks us from our make out session. She pulls away, unlocks the door and pushes it open. Before entering, she whirls around, hand still resting on the doorknob. "Do you want to come in?"

"You know if I come in, it won't be for hand holding and cuddling."

"Good." Her lips curve into a seductive smile. "I hate hand holding and most definitely despise cuddling."

## CHAPTER EIGHT

# WHERE ARE MY PANTS?

## Olivia

With his signature move that I'm growing to love, he grips the back of my neck, and his fingers thread through my hair. He pushes his way through the door as his lips crash to mine. Using his foot he kicks the door, and it slams shut. I moan into his mouth, and he deepens the kiss. He walks me backward, in the dark, until I smack into a solid surface. My hands roam over his chest and shoulders in a frenzy. His tongue caresses mine, soft and seductive. I hike a leg over one of his hips, grinding into him. His bulge hitting me in the right spot causes me to moan. Using the wall for leverage, he hikes up my other leg, and I naturally wrap both around his hips. Now it's his turn to press into me and I whimper. His spicy scent, mixed with a hint of grease, is slowly becoming my new favorite smell.

He pulls away from my lips but continues kissing along my jaw until he reaches my earlobe. "Fuck duchess. I've never been this hard before. All from your sassy mouth," he whispers.

The rough stubble on his cheek scrapes along my heated skin. I throw my head back and moan as my nails dig into his muscular shoulders. Somehow, I remember to use my words. "There's a couch over there. We should go to the couch," I say between pants.

Suddenly, arms wrap around me and I'm no longer leaning against the wall. The porch light casts a warm glow in the formal living room, offering just enough light so Ledger can see where he's going. He falls onto the oversized plush couch, taking me with him so I'm straddling his lap. I roll my hips, so his huge bulge grinds against me on the exact spot I want him. His cheeks are rough and prickly under my fingertips. I would give my left tit to experience the scratching on my inner thighs. Rising on my knees to shift my weight, a slow and seductive voice pours through the speakers. My eyebrows pinch together. For a brief moment, I'm unsure as to what's happening, then I register what's being spoken. "Oh, shit!" I scurry off Ledger's lap. It's not that someone is talking, but my audiobook is playing. My very smutty romance audiobook is playing very loud in my living room.

He laughs. "What is that, and where's it coming from?"

I scramble to turn on a lamp next to the couch. Frantically, I scan the room, searching for the remote. "Stop playing!" I yell while continuing to struggle to find the remote, but the voices don't stop. I dig in the couch cushion as Ledger lifts his leg to get out of my way. My fingers wrap around something solid.

*"Suck on my big, throbbing cock, you dirty girl."*

I freeze. A sheen of sweat covers my forehead. Why is

this happening right now? What did I do to deserve this? I pull out the remote and press the power button. "Why is this piece of junk not working!" Repeatedly, I jab my finger into the button, but instead of turning off, it gets louder.

*"Oh yes, Daddy. Right there. Your cock is so huge it's hitting my cervix. Put your baby in me."*

"Daddy?" He lifts an eyebrow and sits up straighter, wanting to pay closer attention.

I want to find a hole to crawl into. Maybe throw myself off a bridge. Anything would be better than this right now. My cheeks flame red. Dying of embarrassment just might be how I go out. Right now, I'd rather have this happen while stuck in traffic with my windows down. Not now, while making out with a guy I like.

*"Come all over my cock, dirty girl."*

"Why won't this turn off?!" Panic laces my voice. I continue stabbing every button on the remote and nothing is happening. I stomp toward the Wi-Fi device on the media console under the TV, but Ledger's hand on my wrist stops me.

"Wait!"

I twist around and furrow my brows.

His lips turn up into a slow smile. "I kinda want to know if she comes all over his cock."

"Oh my god! You can't be serious?" My heart beats erratically in my chest.

He shrugs. "Might as well see this to the end."

I can't help the laugh that bubbles out of me. Our first somewhat kinda date and we're listening to my romance book. Not only a romance book, but a spicy one and of course it has to play during a sex scene. At this point, there's nothing else I can do. I retreat to the couch and throw myself down next to Ledger. He wraps an arm around my shoulder and holds me tight against him. I drop the remote to my lap, waving the proverbial white flag. We continue listening to the scene until she comes all over his cock and he shoots his orgasm all over her tits and stomach.

"Fuck. Duchess. I have to admit that was pretty hot." He grabs the remote from my lap, pops off the battery cover, and spins the batteries. When he's done, he points the remote at the device and presses the power button. The audiobook stops. No more moans and groans. Only silence fills the room, which isn't any better. I drop my head in my hands.

His hands peel mine away from my face. "Why are you hiding?" His voice is low, but still holds a slight rasp.

"I figure if I hide, you'll just leave and then I won't have to face you." His low chuckle hits me right in the chest.

"I'll let you in on a secret." He grips my chin, forcing me to meet his gaze. "I'm not going anywhere. Don't be embarrassed around me."

I blow out a slow breath and nod. After a few seconds of silence, I ask, "How'd you get the remote to work?"

"You need new batteries. Sometimes you can spin them to get a little more power out of them."

I clench my fist. "Betrayed by batteries," I mumble under my breath. Maybe I should have put the new batteries in the remote instead of my vibrator. But priorities.

"I never would have guessed you like to read smutty books," Ledger says, breaking the silence.

"After a long day, I like to relax and read or listen. Sometimes I lay on the couch and sometimes I draw a bath."

"Maybe I could read or listen with you." He reaches

for my hand, brushing his calloused thumb over my fingers.

"Really? You want to read romance books with me?" I've never been with a guy who's been remotely interested in what I'm reading, let alone want to read them with me. My heart flutters at the thought.

"Sure, why not? Plus, this time he came on her chest. I'm curious if he puts a baby in her." A wide grin covers his face.

"Oh, my god. You're ridiculous." I slap his chest, but he covers my hand with his before I can pull away. He leans over and kisses me. My fingers thread through his dark locks that are held up with a hair tie, wanting to hold him to me. The kiss grows deeper with each passing second.

We shift so I'm lying on the couch cushion and Ledger's body covers mine. He nestles himself between my spread legs. I run my hands over his shoulders, then to his biceps, and down his sides. My fingers clench a handful of his shirt. Lifting my hips, I grind against him. It's been longer than I'd like to admit having a guy between my legs like this. Little pants and moans escape my throat. He trails his fingers over my collarbone, past the hollow beneath my arm, coming inches away from the side of my breast. I arch my back, pushing my chest against him, wanting him to touch me, but he continues to go down, past my ribcage. I whimper when he doesn't touch me where I want him to.

Breaking away from the kiss, I whisper, "Touch me."

"Where do you want me to touch you?"

"Everywhere."

Goosebumps erupt all over my body as his fingers dig under the hem of my shirt, brushing over my bare skin. He runs a finger at the bottom of my bra, tracing the lacy fabric. Then he pulls out and sits up, eyes hooded. The hem of my shirt has ridden up, exposing my bare stomach. His gaze lingers where my shirt meets my skin before his eyes meet mine. I suck my bottom lip into my mouth, nodding at him to do exactly what I know he wants to do. His hands skate over my waist and up past my rib cage, lifting my shirt, revealing my black bra. He rests his palms next to my head, and he bends down, placing open mouth kisses on the swell of one breast, and then the other. I writhe beneath him.

"Mmmm. I love your mouth on me." I run my hands underneath his shirt, salivating at the way his muscles flex and move above me. His mouth covers my nipple over the lace, and I moan. Then he does the same on the other side while he pulls down the cup of my bra, exposing my hard peak to the cool air. He continues to nip and suck, as if he's worshiping each breast.

"Your tits are perfect. Your nipples standing at attention. Begging to be sucked."

"Yes." I moan when he sucks one pebbled nipple into his mouth, his tongue swirling around the peak.

His hand snakes down to the waistband of my jeans and pops the button. Thoughts of having sex with Ledger flash through my mind. I want that so badly, but … My palm pushes on his shoulders, halting his progress.

"This is going to sound odd, but do you mind if we wait to have sex?" His blank stare bores into mine, so I continue. "It's not like I don't want to have sex, because I do. And it's not that I'm a virgin or anything." He quirks an eyebrow at that comment. "I'd just rather wait."

Hell, I don't even know why I want to wait. Normally, I'm the first one tearing my clothes off, but something inside me wants to explore this more without the complications of sex.

"I'm here to do whatever you want. There are other

things we can do." He places open mouth kisses on my chest and up to the column of my neck.

"I like other things." My voice is low and breathy. The delicious scrape of his stubble against my sensitive skin sends goosebumps down my entire body and I can't help but squirm under his touch.

"I could dip my hand into the waistband of your jeans and rub your needy pussy. I bet you're drenched for me."

I moan. "Yes. You should do that."

His hand skates down my stomach until he reaches the open waistband of my jeans. Instinctively, I buck my hips, letting him know exactly what I want.

"Or maybe I'll spread you wide and fuck you with my tongue instead. Lap at your pussy until you're screaming my name."

"Don't tease me." I moan.

He trails kisses down my stomach until he reaches my hips. Peeling away the fabric, he exposes my matching lace panties. With his teeth, he tugs on the strap, releasing it, causing it to snap against my skin. Not hard, but enough to leave a bite. His stormy gaze locks with mine as his thumbs dip into the waistband of my jeans and he tugs down, taking my panties at the same time. I shimmy out of them as he peels them down my legs. Once they're off, he drops them to the floor.

"I want you to come all over my tongue." He winks. His deep voice mimics the male narrator from the audiobook earlier.

He hikes one of my legs over his shoulder. The cool air hits as he spreads me open and I suck in a sharp breath. The flat of his tongue runs up my center. My back arches off the couch as my nails claw at the fabric of the cushion. It's been so long since I've had a guy go down on me, I've forgotten what it's like. Maybe it's like riding a bike, once I experience it again, everything will come rushing back to me. With his thumbs, he spreads me open as he continues to lick me. My moans of pleasure fill the room.

*Yep. There it is.*

"Your pussy is glistening for me. Begging for me to tongue fuck it."

His words cause me to lift my hips, pushing my pussy closer to his mouth. Wanting him to do exactly what he's saying. "Yes! Oh Ledger! Yes."

"Greedy girl." He wraps his lips around my clit and sucks.

My pants and moans grow louder, spurring him to lick faster and suck harder. I brace my palm flat against the couch, but I know I'm going to blast off into space. His thumb circles my clit as his tongue spears into me. I thread a hand into his hair, needing to touch him. To know that he's real, in my living room, about to give me the most explosive orgasm. If the neighbors can hear me screaming out his name through the closed windows, I wouldn't be surprised.

He replaces his tongue with a finger, thrusting in and out. When he pulls out, he adds a second, stretching me even farther. He goes back to sucking and licking my clit. His hand splays across my stomach, trying to hold me still. The contrast of his colorfully inked hand against my untouched skin sends a fireball of heat right between my legs. I never knew I had a thing for tattoos, but apparently they're my kryptonite. With the flick of his tongue, a burst of white dances behind my eyelids. I claw at the couch with one hand, and my nails scrape along his scalp with the other. A delicious tingle flows through my body and I know I'm close. So close.

"Keep going. Oh Ledger. Right there." My chest heaves as I fight to find my breath. He picks up his pace, curling his fingers, hitting my G-spot, and I explode. My orgasm rushes through me like a tsunami. Wave after wave of blissful pleasure. Ledger continues to lap at my wetness, careful not to miss a drop. As I float back down to Earth, he sits up and wipes his mouth with his hand.

"If I had it my way, I'd eat you for every meal." Lust swirls in his gray irises.

"I've never ... I ... just wow." I'm still fighting to catch my breath.

"Speechless again. I'm getting good at this." He grins.

"I've never had an orgasm that intense before. I'm positive I blacked out for a moment."

I attempt to stifle a yawn, but it's useless, and it doesn't go unnoticed. He hops off the couch and I sit back on my elbows, curious about what he's doing. He grabs a blanket off one of the two chairs next to the couch. I rotate to my side to give him room next to me. He covers me with the blanket before laying down and throwing the folded half over himself.

My eyelids fall to half-mast as I fight to keep them open. "I thought you said no cuddling." I rest my cheek on his chest. The steady thumping of his heartbeat lulling me to sleep.

"I'm making an exception." His fingers lazily slide up and down my back until my breathing evens out.

Movement at my side causes me to stir awake. My eyes flutter open, and Ledger is staring at me. Light pours in through the large bay window. Everything from last night flashes through my mind and my lips pull into a slow smile.

"What time is it?"

He brushes a lock of hair off my forehead and tucks it

behind my ear. "It's about 6 a.m. I gotta get going so I can get the shop open."

"Oh. Um. Let me give you a ride to your car." I rise, but he stops me.

"My friend Jay is coming to pick me up."

"Oh. Okay."

"But I'll call you later. And trust me, it'll be before three days."

I exhale a small laugh. "If not, I'll be calling you."

"Deal." He places a soft kiss to my lips, but what I really want to do is tug him to me and continue where we left off last night.

He climbs off the couch, and a few seconds later he's out the front door. I flop onto the cushion. A giddy grin takes over my face. Last night was amazing. It's been so long since I've had an orgasm come remotely close to the one Ledger delivered. A delicious tingle creeps up my spine just thinking about it. I shimmy against the soft fabric as I do a little happy dance. Then I realize I'm still half naked. Where are my pants?

# CHAPTER NINE

# A SEXY SURPRISE

*Olivia*

Over the next week, we've both been so busy we haven't been able to spend any time together. Either I've had late night meetings with my mom, or he's been too tired after work. But somehow, we've managed a few late-night phone calls and the occasional text message throughout the day. There's been a few times when he's been so busy, he's forgotten to eat so I have food delivered to his shop. When he mentioned he was going to be spending his Saturday afternoon there, I had to take matters into my own hands. I'm making sure he gets lunch, plus it's an excuse to see him.

I pull my SUV into an empty spot in front of Ledger's garage. Shutting off the ignition, I grab the brown bag sitting on my passenger seat. I push open the driver's door, the smell of gasoline and motor oil lingering in the air.

I stroll to the gray steel door next to the larger overhead door and pull it open. Music blares through the garage. Good thing I didn't knock, I would have been outside for hours. There's a car raised on jacks in front of one of the tool benches with a light on. If I had to guess, Ledger's working over there. My heels tap on the cement, but with the music, I'm sure anyone who isn't next to me couldn't hear. When I reach the tool bench, I drop the bag on top. Where the hell is he?

Strands of dark hair peek out from underneath the car. I glance down and shriek. My heart nearly leaps out of my chest. Ledger's face and shoulders come into view as he rolls himself out from under the car.

"You scared the shit out of me." My breath is heavy as I clutch my chest.

"Sorry about that. One thing I'm not sorry about is you coming into my shop wearing that dress."

I press the fabric between my legs and squeeze them shut. Heat creeps over my chest and up my neck.

"Don't worry, duchess. Nothing I haven't seen before." Ledger rolls all the way from under the car and rises to his feet. He wipes off his hands, presses a button on a remote, and silence fills the shop. In two steps he's standing in front of me. He grips the nape of my neck, holding me in place while he presses his lips to mine. His fingertips dig into my soft skin, sending a delicious bite through my entire body. This time, my knees clench for a different reason. He breaks away from the kiss, but his grip on my neck doesn't loosen. "What are you doing here?"

I release my hold and my dress floats around my knees. My eyes flutter open and my swollen lips part slightly. This is the first time I've seen him with his hair down. My fingers twitch, wanting to comb through his shoulder length locks. "I came here to see you and make sure you eat, but we can continue with more of the kissing." I rise on my tippy toes and kiss him.

He steps into me, forcing me backward. Then another step. And another. Until my butt hits the edge of the tool bench. I run my hands down his blue button-down work shirt, popping the top button as I work my way down. He deepens the kiss. Hard and possessive. As if it's the only thing worth doing right now. His stomach growls, interrupting my thoughts, and I pull away.

"Sounds like you're hungry."

"I'm hungry for you." He presses a kiss to my cheek, then down to my neck. I shiver from his scratchy scruff. He sucks on my sensitive skin, and I moan.

"No. Let me feed you actual food. I brought some sandwiches." I tilt my head to give him better access while I run my fingers through his hair.

His lips freeze on my neck. He pulls away and peers over my shoulder. "It does smell good."

"Yes. Let's go eat. Then we can continue the neck sucking after." I twist around and pluck the bag off the tool bench. "Where can we eat?"

He pulls an elastic band from his breast pocket and finger combs his hair back, securing it with the band. "Follow me. We'll go to my office."

He grips my hand in his as we walk side by side across the garage and down a short, narrow hallway. He pushes the door the rest of the way open with his foot before flipping on the light switch. The buzz of the fluorescent lights fills the room before it flickers to life. I round the side and hop on the top of his desk. Ledger continues down the hallway and I hear a faucet turning on. When he enters his office, he takes a seat in the leather desk chair. His hands now clean from all the dirt and grease. I cross one leg over my knee, the hem of my dress riding up. I twist at my waist and open the brown bag, pulling out a brown wrapper. Peeling away the paper, I hold out the baguette sandwich to Ledger. He leans in and takes a bite. While he chews, I take a bite of my own.

I moan. "This is so good. Do you like it?"

"Could use some more meat, but it's not bad." He taps my leg to get my attention for another bite and I hold out the sandwich to him.

"I did have them put bacon on it since the gruyere cheese and heirloom tomatoes wouldn't be enough sustenance for you." I continue passing the sandwich between the two of us until it's gone.

"So, what are you working on?" I wipe my hands on a napkin and pass one to Ledger, and he does the same.

"You really want to know? It doesn't seem like your kinda thing."

"Yes! It's part of who you are, and I want to get to know you more."

He raises an eyebrow. "If you want to, but you're not going to understand anything."

"Well, you can teach me." I hop off the desk and straighten my dress. I wrap my fingers around his wrist and tug him out of his seat. Reluctantly, he rises to his feet and trails after me.

Once we reach the garage and are standing next to the car, he grabs another flat thing with wheels and sets it next to the one he was on earlier.

"What's that?" I point to the two rollie things on the floor.

"It's called a creeper. It makes it easier to maneuver around when you're underneath a vehicle. Ladies first." He motions for me to lie down.

I bend at my knees, pressed together and sit sideways to avoid flashing all my lady goods. I squirm back and forth, searching for a good angle to sit on it. When I glance up, Ledger is staring at me with his arms crossed and a smirk on his face.

"Apparently today was not a good day to wear a dress." I shrug.

"That's the reason I avoid wearing one while I work."

"Ha. Ha." Modesty be damned. I haul my other leg over, so my feet are on either side of the creeper. I tug my dress between my legs.

"I won't lie, you look pretty hot like that."

"Just get down here and show me what you're working on."

He chuckles, crouches down, and lays down on his own creeper. "With your feet, push yourself under the car."

Slowly, with one foot I push off and then the other until the underside of the car is above me. "Don't you worry about a car falling on you?"

"Not really."

"Huh? That would be my fear."

He flicks on a light, and the bottom of the car illuminates. "When you know what you're doing, it's not something that crosses your mind. Plus, the ramps are pretty stable and are meant to hold the weight."

"I've never seen what the bottom of a car looks like." I glance around at all the metal and various pipes traveling up and down the length.

"That doesn't surprise me."

I turn my head and give him a snarky smile.

He moves the treble light around the underside of the car pointing out basic parts and explaining what they are and what they're for. Dirt and grease cover his hand as he touches all the various parts. Then he shines the light on a front tire. "You see this part?"

"Yeah."

With his other hand, he reaches up and wiggles a long bar that connects the tire to the car. "This is called a tie rod. You see how it moves?"

"Let me guess, it's not supposed to."

"Correct. It should be solid and stiff."

"Me and the car have something in common." He glances my way. "I like things solid and stiff too." A playful smile flirts on my lips. I glide my hand up his denim covered thigh until I'm cupping his impressive bulge even when he's not hard.

He exhales a grunt when I give him a gentle squeeze. "Is that so?" he asks, his voice low and gravelly.

My teeth sink into my lower lip and nod. Suddenly, he's scooting himself out from under the car. A few seconds later, a pair of hands grip my ankles and tug. I yelp in surprise. When the overhead lights of the garage come into view, an angry Ledger stares down at me, nostrils flaring. Maybe it's more lust filled anger. Either way, it causes goosebumps to creep up my arms and my nipples to pebble beneath my dress. I rise to my feet and stand in front of him. Steely gray eyes bore into mine and my chest heaves with every passing second.

Finally, he breaks the silence. "How much do you like this dress?" He nods at my bone-colored Michael Kors Belted Utility Dress.

I glance down. "I have no attachment to it. It's last seas—"

"Good. Then you won't mind if I dirty you up." He wraps an arm around my waist, his hand splayed out across my ass, and hauls me to him.

"I like when you make me dirty."

Then his lips are on mine. Full of heat and passion. He guides me backward until my butt hits his tool bench. Without breaking our kiss, he grips my waists and lifts me so sitting on top. My dress hikes up as I spread my legs, inviting him closer. His hands roam up my thighs, over my rib cage. The scruff on his jaw is prickly under my fingertips. Reaching around, I find the elastic tie holding his hair up and tug. When his locks fall free, I run my hands through the strands, loving the softness between my fingers. A groan rumbles from his throat when I grip a hand full of his hair, deepening the kiss. He glides his hands down to my waist and then to the top of my thighs. He breaks our kiss and we both glance down. A smeared grease handprint covers the light-colored fabric.

"Now I can see all the places you've touched me."

"Yep." His warm lips press against my neck.

I tilt my head to give him better access. "Is it strange that it turns me on?"

He stops. His breath skates across my heated skin. "Me touching you or my dirty handprint?"

I purse my lips, thinking about my answer. "Both."

"Whatever you like, I'm here for it." He goes back to kissing and nipping my neck. Then he pulls away and flicks the top button of my dress open. He continues his way down to the second and then the third until the sides fold over, exposing my light pink lace bra. Bending down, he places hot, open mouth kisses along my collarbone. Then he trails kisses to the swell of my breasts. His scuff tickles my sensitive skin. I moan out his name and spread my legs wider, wrapping my heels around his butt and tugging him closer, needing more of him. He continues to nip and suck on my skin. I move my hands between us and pop the button of his pants. The zipper slides down when I tug on one side. I shove my hand inside and run my hand down his length over his boxer briefs. When I run my hand up, my thumb rubs over the head and I freeze. I run my thumb over the head one more time, just to confirm. I pull away and shove his shoulders. His eyebrows pinch together.

"Are you … pierced? A Prince Albert?"

His lips tip up to one side. "Yeah."

I bite my lip, a shy smile fighting to take over. "I want to see."

He takes a step backward and holds his hands out, offering me free rein to check him out. When I don't move, he nods in encouragement.

My eyes go wide like a kid on Christmas Day. Hunched over, I peel away his pants like I'm ripping open my very own special present. I'm not a prude by any means. I've seen my fair share of cocks. In person and watching porn. I've seen pierced ones in videos, but this is the first time I'm seeing one up close and personal. I slide my hands into the waistband of his boxer briefs and slowly push them down in hopes I don't hurt anything. Once the elastic is past his hips, his very impressive cock springs free. By the looks of it, he's only half hard. On the very tip is a shiny silver ball, and another ball sits on top at the base of his head. Slowly, I drag my thumb over the ball on the tip. Ledger inhales a sharp breath through his teeth and his cock twitches.

"Is it sensitive?"

"When you keep playing with it."

"Sorry." I continue slowly stroking him up and down, being careful of the two balls.

"If you don't stop, I'm going to blow my load all over your dress."

"Well, you already ruined my dress, so might as well see this to the end." I increase the pressure of my grip. I love the feel of him in my hand. Then my mind wanders to what it would be like to have him inside me. Stretching me. Imagining what his piercing would feel like inside of me. My heels dig into his ass, pulling him closer.

When I glance up, Ledger's hooded eyes are watching my every movement. Every slow stroke. My tongue peeks out and his gaze follows as I lick my bottom lip. Suddenly, his hand comes up and grips the nape of my neck, hauling me to him until our lips crash together in a bruising kiss. I moan into his mouth, and he deepens the kiss. Our tongues stroke and caress each other. My grip on his cock tightens as I continue to stroke him. His breathing grows heavy. His hips push forward into my grip.

"Oh. Fuck. That feels so good." His head rolls back, soaking up my touch, before falling forward. He's transfixed on my fingers as they wrap around him, pumping him up and down. As I quicken my strokes, his grunts grow more intense, echoing through the air. "I can't hold on much longer." His thrust grows more frantic.

"Make me dirty." My tongue peeks out, wetting my lips. I want to watch him come in my hand. My mind drifts off, wondering what it would be like to have his piercing scraping the roof of my mouth.

"Fuuuck." His orgasm rips through him as ribbons of cum splatter on my dress. Spurt after spurt, until his movements slow, eventually coming to a stop. Glancing down, a splatter of wet spots cover the front of my dress.

He cups my cheeks, forcing me to meet his eyes. "You can come surprise me at the shop anytime you want." Before I can respond, he kisses me, except this time it's short.

While he tucks himself back into his jeans, I say, "I figured I owed you one after the night on my couch."

Wordlessly, he rips off a sheet of a blue towel from the roll and cleans himself off my dress. Or the best he can, but mostly he just smears it in.

"It's okay. I'm going home after this, anyway." I grab the rag from him.

"Hold on."

Ledger turns around, his long strides carry him across the garage, and then he disappears down the hallway we entered earlier. A minute later, he returns, a dark blue cloth in his hand. When he's standing in front of me, he holds out a button-down work shirt. On the left side there's a white patch with his name embroidered on it.

"You can wear this." A sheepish smile appears on his face. "At least it's clean. And you don't have to go home looking like Monica Lewinsky."

I laugh and shake my head. I unbutton the front of my dress and it falls to the floor. He holds out his shirt for me as I put one arm in the hole and then the other. His shirt is huge on me. The bottom reaches my mid thighs, so it's only a little shorter than my dress. I push each button through their corresponding hole. Once I'm finished, I do a twirl and hold a pose. "How do I look?"

Ledger eyes me from head to toe. "New fantasy. You in nothing but my work shirt."

# CHAPTER TEN

# TEAM LEDGER

*Olivia*

"You're walking a little bow legged. You and Ledger have some fun last night." Tatum eyes me warily before wrapping her arms around me for a hug. When we break away, she pulls out her chair and I pull out mine. The quaint café is quiet this morning, so it doesn't take long to get our order. Aside from the days we get together with friends, Tatum and I always plan a few hours for just the two of us. Call it sisterly bonding.

Ledger and I have been determined to see each other more than once a week. We'll do whatever it takes to make it happen. It might be a mid-day rendezvous, or an after work bite to eat. He's come over to my place a few times and I've made him dinner. We'd relax on the couch together afterward and one of us would end up falling asleep. Of course, this is after exchanging orgasms. Maybe it was the orgasm coma that made us so tired. Last night was no different. He bent me over the arm of the couch with his mouth between my legs. Which is a completely different experience than when he's on top. My other senses were heightened since I couldn't see what he was doing. Instead, I had to experience how he lazily dragged the head of his cock up and down my slick pussy, the silver ball on the tip hitting my clit, which sent a delicious shiver up my spine. But he never entered me, not with his dick, at least. My thighs clench together just thinking about it.

"No." A warm blush covers my cheeks and I drop my gaze, avoiding eye contact. While we didn't have sex, we both saw stars. I most likely passed out sometime after.

"That look is telling me that no means yes. Spill it. How good was it?" The server arrives just at that moment and sets our coffees down on the table.

I lean in so no one else can hear. "The things he does, it's like I don't ever need sex again. My life would be one-hundred percent complete with the way he strums my clit."

Her eyes go wide. "Wait? You two haven't had sex yet? Because that's not like you."

I nibble on my thumbnail. "I told him I wanted to wait, and I don't know why. The first time we kissed, something felt different. But mind blowing different. I want to explore those feelings more before sex complicates it." My sister knows me better than anyone, including my relationships, and she's right. It's not like me. But I want to try something new since what I was doing before clearly wasn't working anymore.

"How does sex complicate it? To me, it sounds like a good time." She takes a sip of her coffee.

"Only because you've been with your boyfriend for years and you know all there is to know about each other."

Tatum met her boyfriend after they hired her at his law firm as an office administrator. "I'm still exploring. I have my treasure map and now I just need to find the X."

"Well, you already found the O. Only a few more letters until you get to the X."

We both laugh. "I just want to take our time. Get to know each other."

"Did you have them put Bailey's in your coffee?" Tatum reaches across the table for my coffee mug and lifts it up to her nose for a whiff.

"Ha ha. No. I'm just trying something different this time." I steal my mug back from her grip.

"So, you're telling me he's been inside you? Just not with his penis?"

My cheeks flush and I nod. "Several times."

"You have more willpower than me. I'd be itching to find out what he's packing underneath his ripped jeans and Henley's."

"Trust me, I know what's underneath. I just haven't had the full Ledger experience yet."

"It's kinda odd that he's so not your type. In fact, he's like the complete opposite of your type. If your type is here," she holds out one hand at one end of the table then points away from us, "he's in the building across the street."

Dropping my head to my open palm that's propped up on the table, I exhale a sigh. "I know. I know. He just makes me feel … different. But a good kind of different. Maybe I needed a change to get me out of this dating rut." He throws my entire world off axis. Give me a guy in a suit and tie and I know exactly what to do, but give me a guy with tattoos and a man bun and I'm a flustered mess.

"So, get him out of your system and then find someone else?" She takes a bite of her blueberry scone.

"What's with all these questions?" I break off a piece of my cranberry lemon muffin and pop it into my mouth.

"Answering my question with a question, I see how it is. Well, I ask because you'll need a date to Mom's ballroom charity event."

"Oh shit, I forgot about that." This is just one of many charity events my mom organizes. Tatum and I always help her with all her events, but lately I've been so caught up with Ledger I spaced on what day it is.

"Are you taking Ledger with you? Mom would have a heart attack." She breaks off a piece of her scone.

"I don't want to subject him to that level of craziness. Plus, I'm sure he wouldn't be interested, anyway." I wave my hand, dismissing the thought. "I'll find someone to go with me. That way, I don't have to be set up by Mom."

"How is that going for you? Did she introduce you to the new lawyer in town? Apparently, he joined the country club and from what I hear, she's been talking you up." She gives me a devilish smile.

"Ugh." I roll my eyes. "No. Why can't she stop meddling and let me find my own dates?"

"You know she won't do that until you're walking down the aisle and popping out a baby. Hopefully not at the same time."

"She needs to focus on her own life and stop worrying about mine."

She shrugs. "Mom lives to meddle, so that's never going to happen."

I sigh. Unfortunately, it's the truth. Once she gets her way, she finds something new to fixate on. For a month straight, she hounded me about dying my hair to have a fresh, new look. "I could ask Trey. He'd be a good choice. Plus, Mom has always loved him, so I know he'd have her approval. Forget the American dream. The actual dream is to have Mom's approval." The sarcasm is clear in my tone.

We finish our coffee and pastries, and I order a couple of breakfast sandwiches to bring to Ledger on my way home. Plus, it's another excuse to see him.

I drive to the other side of town to make an unannounced stop at Ledger's shop. When I walk inside, he's lowering a car to the ground with one of the lifts. A spark of hope ignites inside me. Maybe he's finished for the day and we can spend some time together.

"Hey, how's it going?" The clacking of my heels against the cement draws his attention.

His gaze peers over at me and never leaves mine until the car is on the ground. "What do I owe this pleasure?"

"I just finished breakfast with my sister and thought I would drop by." Once I'm standing in front of him, my heart hammers in my chest. "Have I ever told you how sexy you look in your mechanic shirt with grease smeared on your hands?"

"I still attest that you look a hell of a lot better in my shirts than I do." His gaze lingers on mine as if he's debating if he wants to eat the sandwich or me. With his hooded eyes, I vote me. "Come on, let's go to my office."

It's me! It's me! Good thing I put on my lucky lace thong this morning.

He grabs the bag from my hands. "This smells delicious."

A pang of disappointment flits through me, but I'm careful to not let it show. He wants the actual meal and not the *me* meal.

He bends down and kisses me, careful not to get his

grease covered hands on my outfit this time. I've ruined three dresses because of him but let me say, each time was totally worth it.

On our way to his office, he pauses at a utility sink to scrub his hands with Orange Goop. Supposedly, it's better for getting the grease off, but from his years of working, he has permanently stained fingertips. After his hands are clean, or as clean as they can be, he pulls me to him for a proper kiss. His warm body presses against mine as his fingers dig into my waist. These are the moments I love. Being wrapped in his arms with his lips on mine. It's sweet, but sensual at the same time. Kissing him is quickly becoming my favorite pastime. When we break apart, he leads me the rest of the way to his office. He takes a seat behind the desk, and I take my usual spot on the desktop facing him.

"How was breakfast with your sister?" he asks as he unravels the top of the bag and pulls out a bagel sandwich.

"It was good. She reminded me of a charity gala I totally forgot about coming up in a couple of weeks." I contemplate if I should invite Ledger. But his wandering gaze makes me change my mind. It's not his type of thing so I'm sure he won't want to go, anyway. These are black tie events and I highly doubt he even owns a tie, let alone a suit. Trey would be a more logical choice. Plus, socializing is more his speed and I know he has a closet full of suits.

"That sounds like a fun time," he deadpans.

Moving on to a more neutral topic, I ask, "So, what are you doing for the rest of the day?"

"I'm finished in the shop, but I do need to go grocery shopping. I think the milk in my fridge has turned into cottage cheese." He takes a bite of his sandwich.

My nose scrunches. "That's gross. But I love shopping.

And I have nothing going on for the rest of the day, so I'll come with you."

"You enjoy grocery shopping?" He drops his sandwich and rests his elbows on the desk. "Like the people who insist on stopping in the middle of the aisle so no one can walk past them? Or others who walk so slow as if they're on a Sunday drive enjoying the scenery?"

I lift one shoulder and let it drop. "I enjoy every kind of shopping."

He barks out a laugh and leans back in his chair. "Sure. I won't say no to the company."

My eyes light up, and I hop off the desk, tugging on his arm with all my might. "Then let's go."

"But I'm still eating."

"Finish it in the car."

He snatches his half-eaten sandwich off the paper wrapper and I lead him out of his office.

"Do I want the spicy mustard or the stone-ground mustard?" He holds a bottle in each hand, weighing his options.

"It's mustard. It can't be that difficult of a decision."

"This condiment choice could make or break my dinner. It's a decision that can't be made lightly." He reads the label of one bottle and then the other.

I pluck both bottles from his hands and toss them into his cart. "Whenever I'm faced with a tough decision like this, I get both." He shrugs and pushes the cart forward. I whirl around and pluck a bottle off the shelf and hold it out to him. "What about ketchup?"

"What about it?" His eyebrows pinch together.

"Do you want some?"

"No." His tone is stern, as if ketchup has wronged him in the past. Like a scorned ex-lover.

"You don't like ketchup?"

"Nope."

"How can you not like ketchup?" I grip my waist and pop my hip.

"Because it exists."

His face is void of any emotion. Stone cold serious. I can't help but bust out laughing right in the middle of aisle four.

"You think it's funny, but I'm serious."

"I just ... I've never ... I don't even know what to say to that." I double over, holding my stomach from laughing so hard.

"Facts."

Ledger continues to push the cart down the aisle, and I trail behind him, trying to compose myself. We round the corner, and our cart collides with another shopper. I peer up and apologize to the woman with dark brown hair with a few strands of gray on the sides.

"Ledger. It's so good to see you." The older woman rounds the cart and wraps her arms around him. All I can do is stare at what's happening in front of me as he wraps one arm around her shoulder in return. She knows his name, so he's not wrapping his arms around a random stranger because I know that's something he'd never do. Something about her is familiar like she reminds me of someone, but I can't put my finger on it. When they separate, her gaze meets mine and returns to Ledger. "And who is this beautiful lady?"

Before Ledger can say anything, I hold out my hand for her. "Hi. I'm Olivia."

"I don't do handshakes. I hug." Within seconds, she's

pulling me into a tight hug, similar to the one she gave to Ledger. "I'm Mona. Ledger's stepmom."

"It's a pleasure to meet you, Mona." I give her a warm smile.

"Likewise, dear. It's nice to see Ledger out," she shields her mouth from Ledger with her hand, "with a woman. It's been a while."

Ledger rolls his eyes. "You know you're not being very secretive. I can still hear you."

"Well good. Then you know how excited I am. You know, we're doing dinner next Sunday. Everyone is coming over. You two should join us."

Ledger rubs the back of his neck with his hand. "I'm not sure that's such a great idea."

"Nonsense. It's been ages since you've come over. Olivia can come too." Her gaze darts to me as if I'm the one who holds all the decision making power. Ledger and I have only known each other for about a month and I'm being asked to meet the parents. But the puppy dog look on Mona's face tells me I better agree to this, or it might break her heart. And I'm not one to be breaking hearts.

"We'd love to," I blurt out.

Ledger glares at me, wide eyed, and all I can do is shrug.

"That's so wonderful. I can't wait to tell your father." Mona rises to her tippy toes and places a kiss on Ledger's cheek. Then she's pulling me into another tight hug. "I'll let you two finish. We'll see you next Sunday."

Once Mona rounds the corner of the aisle with her cart, Ledger turns to me. "You don't know what you've just done."

"Accepted an invitation to your parents for dinner?" I rest my hand on my chest. "Parents love me. What could go wrong? It's not like I opened Pandora's box. Or a portal to hell."

Ledger barks out a humorless laugh and shakes his head as he continues pushing the cart down the aisle.

I trail after him. "If you're nervous about what your family will think of me, you have absolutely nothing to worry about."

"It's not that. We're not exactly *The Brady Bunch*."

I come to a stop next to him. "Whatever happens, I'm always on Team Ledger."

## CHAPTER ELEVEN

# DIDN'T GO AS EXPECTED

*Olivia*

My stomach is a ball of knots. Parents love me. I shouldn't have anything to worry about, but currently I'm worrying about anything and everything. I've changed my outfit ten times. At first my hair was up, then I thought better of it and put it down. I've changed my earrings three times, but who's counting. I want everything to be perfect. What if they don't like me and, in turn, Ledger decides not to like me? He doesn't seem like the kind of guy to be like that. At least, based on the earlier interaction with Mona. What if he's changed his mind and wants his parents' approval and I'm not what they want for their son? I've never been this much of a hot mess before, and I don't know how to deal. Most of the time, I'm already well acquainted with any parents because they know mine, but this is different. I guess I wanted different.

I run my clammy palms down my denim skinny jeans as I stare out the window of Ledger's black Silverado. Tall pines zip past us. Ledger brakes, slowing down before turning left onto a paved driveway. We snake our way up to the house when several cars come into view parked along the side. I do a double take when I catch sight of a black SUV.

No way. That can't be his. There are plenty of black Escalades in the city. Then my gaze falls on a sticker on the rear window.

## SBL
## Single Bros Life.

*Son of a bitch.*

Suddenly, I'm no longer nervous about meeting the parents, but who else is in the house? Maybe one of his friends also drives a black Escalade. It's not a super uncommon car.

Ledger comes to a stop in front of the garage and shuts off the ignition. He releases his seat belt, but I don't move.

"Um. Do you think this is a good idea? Maybe we should do this some other time."

He tilts his head in my direction. "You seemed pretty excited when Mona suggested we come. You can't back out now. I'm sure she's watching us out the window as we speak."

I glance up to the large picture window and notice the curtains rustling, like someone was just watching from the window. I swallow hard, my throat feeling dry. I've always been told to face my fears, but I don't think this is what they meant.

Hesitantly, I unbuckle my seat belt and push open the door and Ledger does the same. With a deep breath, I reach around to the backseat, and grab the bottle of wine I brought for dinner. As I push the door shut, I contemplate if I should open this bottle and chug it in the driveway. Before I can do just that, I glance up and Ledger's waiting for me in front of his truck. I collect my bearings and make my way toward him.

"Ready?" He holds out his hand for me.

All I can do is nod my head because no, I am not ready. Moisture collects on my palms. I wipe them on my thighs, but it's useless. We walk side by side, fingers intertwined, up to the front door. Ledger peers down at me and I give him an apprehensive smile. I wish I knew what I was walking into right now.

Before we can knock, the front door flies open. Mona stands in the doorway, a beaming smile on her face. She holds out her arms and wraps Ledger in a hug. Then she offers me the same greeting and it eases some of my worries.

*See, nothing to worry about. Parents love you.*

"I'm so happy the two of you could make it. I was a little nervous that maybe I was too forward when I ran into you two." Mona ushers us through the doorway, where it opens to a large foyer. A set of stairs run along the wall to the right leading up to the second floor. A formal living room is on the left. The cream walls give it an elegant style, but not too stuffy. This is not a place I can picture Ledger living in. If anything is out of place, it's him. Straight ahead is a hallway that opens into the kitchen. Mona moves next to me and leads us down the hallway.

Earlier in the week, I asked Ledger about his family, but he was pretty tight-lipped. All he mentioned was his dad, Kenny, stepmom Mona, and that he has a couple of half siblings. He didn't seem too eager to share more, so I didn't want to push it. When I asked about his mom, he completely shut me out. I figured he'll tell me when he's ready.

"Not forward at all. Thank you for the invite." It was a little forward, but I won't tell her that. She was just excited to see her stepson, and apparently with a woman.

"Of course. I don't remember the last time Ledger came over for dinner. We've invited him several times, but he always said he was busy working in the garage," Mona says.

"Is that so?" I spare a glance at Ledger and he shrugs his shoulders.

As we step through the stone arched doorway and into the kitchen, I first notice an older man standing on one side of the island. He's in his early sixties and has a striking resemblance to Ledger. Strong jaw. Straight nose. He holds out his hand and introduces himself as Kenny. On the other side are two other people, both appear to be in their early twenties. With a quick wave, they introduce themselves as Ava and Liam. Then a familiar face, one I was crossing my fingers that I wouldn't see, rounds the corner.

"Olivia? What are you doing here?" Trey takes a few steps until he's standing in front of me. His arms wrap me up in a bear hug. I can't move. One he's gripping me so tight. And two, I'm frozen in shock. "If you wanted to see me, all you needed to do was call. You didn't have to show up at my parents' house. But also, how did you know where my parents live?"

"She's with me." Ledger's voice is deep and gravelly. When I glance his way, his jaw clenches, like if Trey doesn't release me, he might force him to … with his fist.

Trey's grip around me loosens, but he doesn't fully let

FLIRTING WITH THE BAD BOY

me go. He glances down at me. I give him a tight smile and nod in confirmation. His arm drops to his side, and he takes a step back. Ledger locks eyes with Trey as he moves to stand next to me, wrapping an arm around my shoulder.

"So, this might be obvious now, but how do you two know each other?" Deep down, I hope they're neighbors and Trey's just stopping by, or maybe a distant cousin who comes over for dinner, anything but—

"He's my brother," Trey deadpans.

*Shit. Not what I wanted to hear.*

"Half-brother," Ledger corrects. "Same dad. Different moms."

That explains why Mona looked so familiar. She and Trey share the same facial features.

"So what's going on here? Are you two … together?" Trey points between the two of us.

"Yes." Ledger's grip on me tightens.

"No," I say at the same time as Ledger. We glance at each other. "We're seeing where it goes." I shrug.

"Huh?" Trey's eyebrows knit together. There's a moment of silence. "Well, you always did like my sloppy seconds."

"Trey!" Mona screeches.

Ledger drops his arm from around me and takes a step toward Trey. "What does that mean?"

"Excuse me?!" I slide past Ledger because there's no shoving him, and stalk toward Trey.

Trey narrows his eyes at me. "You didn't tell your boy toy we kissed."

"Why would I have told him we kissed, when I didn't even know you two knew each other? And he's not my boy toy. Also, I am no one's sloppy seconds!" My palms shove into Trey's chest, but he barely moves a step. My entire body trembles with rage. This is supposed to be my best friend, and he's treating me like one of his dirty one-night stands. The urge to punch him is strong, but since I've never punched anyone, I do the next best thing. I twist around and pluck a dinner roll out of a basket on the kitchen island and hurl it at his head. Trey ducks. The dinner roll grazes the hair on the top of his head. I take a second shot with another roll. This time, it hits him right in the forehead.

"What the hell? Why are you throwing food at me?" Trey yells.

I clench my fists. "Because you basically called me a whore!" I twist around to get another roll, but Ledger pushes the basket just out of reach.

"Because you're with him!" He points a finger at Ledger.

This time Ledger shoulders past me and gets in Trey's face. "Why the fuck do you care? You mad she chose me over you? Kinda like when Candy picked me over you. How does it feel being second best?"

"Fuck you! She only crawled to you because I was done with her." Trey shoves Ledger, who only stumbles back a few inches. "Amanda, Sara … I can keep going. You took in all my discarded trash. Look at her. There's no reasonable explanation for her to be with a guy like you."

"Someone who's not a prick? Someone who doesn't look like he's got a stick shoved so far up his ass he looks like a puppet in a suit? You're just pissed I won. She chose the better man." Ledger is inches from Trey's face.

"Okay! That's enough, you two," Mona yells, but it goes unnoticed.

Trey lets out a menacing laugh. "You don't think she has a taste for the expensive? I guarantee you she'd rather have Dom Perignon than Boone's Farm."

Ledger shakes his head. "Let me guess, I'm the Boons Farm?"

"If the fruit on the label fits …"

I grab the nearest glass with liquid in it and throw it in his face. Droplets of what smells like wine, run down his face. His light gray shirt turning charcoal. "Fuck you, Trey!" I seethe. "I'm no one's sloppy seconds, no one's trash. And most of all you have zero say about my love life."

He wipes a hand down his face. "I figured you'd have better taste than him."

"How do you know what I like? You know what? Don't answer that. I'm out of here." I sidestep Trey and Ledger. "Sorry, Mona and Kenny. I'd like to say we'll do this again, but I don't think that'll happen."

I step up to Ledger, so we are toe to toe. My voice low. "I'm not a trophy to be won. You two want to fight about it, fine. But I don't want to be involved."

Without sparing a glance behind me, I storm out of the house. My heartbeat pounds in my ears as my hands tremble. All my emotions bubble over until everything finally explodes. Tears run down my cheeks. I brush them away but it doesn't matter, they keep pouring down. I hear the front door open, and I spare a glance over my shoulder. Ledger's standing in the doorway, hurt and confusion etched on his face, but he doesn't say anything. He doesn't come after me. And that might be the thing that hurts the most.

# CHAPTER TWELVE

# WASN'T MEANT TO BE

*Ledger*

I run out the front door but stop before I reach the driveway. So much for being Team Ledger. It's better this way. Trey's right. We don't belong together. You can't force water and oil to mix. And that's exactly what we are. We don't mix. She's a ray of sunshine and I'm the dark cloud that will only hold her back. Our lives are too different.

"We put up with a lot of this fighting while you and Trey grew up. But I was hoping since you two are adults, you'd put your differences aside for one meal, but clearly, I was wrong." Mona comes to stand next to me.

"That's why I didn't want to come. It's best I stay away. Sorry I came." I storm toward my truck.

"Ledger. Ledger! That's not what I meant!" Mona yells.

As I open the driver's door, a hand clutches my forearm. I twist around to find Trey standing there. I yank my arm from his grasp. "Don't worry, I'm leaving."

"What are you doing with Olivia?" He narrows his eyes.

"Why the fuck does it matter?" I spit out.

"She's one of my best friends and I hate to see her get caught up in what bullshit you got going on in your life."

"Like what? Busting my ass working? Making a living for myself? Because whatever you think my life is about, is not it. In fact, you know nothing about me. So why don't you go back inside, and everyone can go back to being one big happy family. Without me." I climb up into my truck and pull the door shut, but his grip on the frame stops me.

"She deserves the best."

His words sting as if I'm not the one who can give it to her. And he's probably right. I'll never be able to give her everything she deserves. Not even a fraction of it. It's better that I come to grips with that now, instead of after we get too deep.

"And apparently, that's not me." I tug on the door again, and Trey lets go before his fingers get crushed. Turning over the ignition, I pop it into reverse. When I reach the end of the driveway, the tires squeal as I race down the road, hoping I can find Olivia. At the very least, I can give her a ride home. I don't want her walking the secluded country roads. A mile down the road, when I don't spot her, I make a U-turn in a driveway and search for her in the other direction, but nothing. There's no way she could have gotten far. Pulling out my phone, I dial her number. It rings a few times, then goes to voicemail. I try again. Same thing. This time I leave a message. A few seconds later, a text message pops up.

OLIVIA

I'm fine.

She says she's fine, but I don't believe it because I know I'm far from fine.

# CHAPTER THIRTEEN

# THE WRONG GROVELER

*Olivia*

When I reach the end of the driveway, I call Charlie. Luckily, she's only five minutes away and can pick me up. I continue walking toward the setting sun. Never in my wildest dreams would I suspect Trey and Ledger are brothers. Or half-brothers. They are complete opposites. Now that I think about it, they both have the same steely gray eyes. This is an absolute mess. And poor Mona. She must hate me. I yelled, swore, and threw food at what was supposed to be a nice family dinner. Thankfully, it was white wine instead of red that I threw on Trey. I make note to send apology flowers and a cleaning service for the mess I made.

The crunching of gravel draws my attention. I glance up and Charlie's SUV comes into view as she pulls up next to me with the window rolled down. "This seems only fitting that I finally get to return the favor." Her long brown hair flows down her shoulders as she leans cross the center console, a smirk playing on her lips.

I give her a crooked smile before opening the door and climbing in. There was a time when Charlie stormed out of Bennett's house, and she called me to pick her up on the side of the road.

She steps on the gas, but keeps her gaze trained on the blacktop in front of us. "So, what happened?"

I sigh. "It was a disaster. Think of the worst possible thing that could happen and times it by ten."

Charlie peers at me. "What happened?"

"Let's start big." I clap my hands in front of me like an enthusiastic cheerleader. Too bad this pep rally is more like a dumpster fire. "Did you know Trey has siblings?"

"I know he's mentioned a younger brother and sister. But what does this have to do with Trey?"

A humorless laugh bubbles out of me. "Oh, the fun part, Ledger is also Trey's brother. Well, half-brother. But they are definitely related."

The car jerks to the left, and my hands fly to the dashboard. "The guy you've been hooking up with is Trey's brother?!" Charlie screeches.

"Yep." I pop the p at the end.

"Oh. Shit. What are you going to do?" Her gaze darts between me and the road.

"I can't even wrap my head around everything. Trey said some pretty hurtful things. And I'm sure it was all in the heat of the moment, but they hurt nonetheless. Ledger seemed more interested in arguing with Trey. Everything's just a mess." Right now, I'm seething at the both of them and at myself. I'm so embarrassed this all happened in front of his parents. In their home. Yeah, they are never inviting me over again.

She reaches over and rests her hand on my knee, giving it a gentle squeeze. "I'm sure you'll figure it out."

I blow out a breath. "Yeah. Right now, I can't bear to talk to either of them."

My phone rings and Ledger's name flashes across the screen. I send it right to voicemail, but he calls again. I don't answer, but he leaves a message.

"Who's that?" She nods at my phone in my lap.

"Ledger. He's wondering where I am."

"You better let him know you're okay, at least. I'd hate for him to think someone kidnapped you or something."

"Yeah. You're right." I type out a reply, hit send, and shove my phone into my pocket. Even though I'd rather have him stew about it for a while.

The rest of the car ride is silent as I stare out the window. For once, everything in my life was going well. So, of course, it just couldn't stay that way.

When Charlie pulls into my driveway, I hop out and tell her I'll call her later. I need time to digest everything. Alone. As soon as I enter my house, Charlie reverses out. The door closes behind me with a click and I exhale a sigh, the wood door cool against my back. A pint of rocky road, yoga pants, and a romantic comedy are exactly what I need to forget about the day. My phone buzzes in my pocket. I pull it out, see the name on the screen, and roll my eyes. I press silent, not wanting to talk to my mom right now. As soon as the buzzing stops, it starts up again. Knowing I can't ignore her any longer because she'll continue calling or worse, show up here, I answer.

"Hi Mom." Annoyance laces my tone.

"Is that how you greet your mother?"

"I'm not really in the mood. What do you want?" I push off the door and amble toward my kitchen.

"You don't need to be so rude. I raised you better than that."

I roll my eyes. "What can I help you with?" I give her my best fake retail voice.

"Have you found a date for the charity gala yet?"

"Really? This is why you're calling me right now? Why is it such a big deal if I bring a date?" I open the fridge and pull out a half empty bottle of wine.

"Your sister is bringing her boyfriend. I would hate for you to feel left out."

"I'm absolutely fine with it. But it appears you're not." I pull out the temporary stopper and set it on the counter. Glancing around, I find a wine glass, but it's on the other side of the kitchen. I eye the glass, then the bottle. Fuck it. I bring the bottle to my lips and tip it back, swallowing a large gulp.

"Nonsense. Dr. Reinhart has a son who's also a pediatrician and single. I'll set you two up."

If the son is anything like his dad, his hair is receding and he smells like latex. I'd rather go alone. Or not at all. "I'll be sure to find a date," I say. I don't know where, but anyone will be better than doctor latex.

"Okay. But if you need me to set you up, just say the word. Also, remember Monday we have to meet with the caterers to finalize the menu."

"Yeah, I'll be there right when I'm finished with work."

I guzzle down another swig of wine.

Monday morning, I arrive at my desk to a massive bouquet of white Asiatic lilies, yellow roses, blue delphiniums, and purple monte casinos. I stick my nose to the blooms and inhale their sweet floral scent. For a moment, my heart leaps out of my chest until I find the card and pull it out to see they're from Trey. It's not that I'm disappointed they're from Trey and he's apologizing. I just wish someone else would have sent them. Like a certain bad boy who I haven't heard from since the voicemail he left after the incident at his parents'. Pulling out my phone, I send a quick message to Trey thanking him for the flowers but I'm still mad at him. Throughout the day, my phone pings with messages and each time I'm disappointed they're not from Ledger but instead from Trey telling me how sorry he is. Which also included several selfies of himself with captions that say how sad he is that I'm mad at him. He even had lunch delivered from my favorite Japanese restaurant along with a gift certificate for a day at the spa. By the end of the workday, I think Trey spent more time groveling instead of working so I put him out of his misery and tell him while I'm still hurt, I do accept his apology. But the thing that hurts the most is I didn't receive a single message or a missed call from Ledger.

After work, I pull into the parking lot of 218 Market. They're known for their local cuisines with a modern twist. As I walk through the double wood doors, I'm greeted by the hostess and let her know I'm meeting with the caterers. With how many times I've been here, I'm surprised they don't know me by name. She leads me into the dining room. The warm glow of the evening sun shines in through a one hundred and eighty degree half circle window wall that overlooks Lake Superior. Immediately, I spot my mom sitting next to Tatum. She's very animatedly telling them what she expects for this event. This is nothing new. She always strives for perfection, not only for her events, but for her children as well.

When I reach the table, my mom directs her attention to me. "Olivia. Finally, you're here. I was wondering if you were going to show up or if it would have been another flat tire incident. Hurry, take a seat. You've missed so much already."

Tatum slides over in the high back leather booth. I press a button on my phone and the time illuminates the screen. "I'm only five minutes late. Plus, I was at work, and I can't predict what the traffic's going to be like."

She rolls her eyes before going back to dictating to the caterers how she wants the food displayed.

Once I'm seated, Tatum leans in and whispers, "I would have faked the flat. This meeting is brutal. I'm pretty sure I've seen tears well up in this poor woman's eyes at least five times now."

"So, Mom's in a mood. Great. That means she'll be on my case as soon as this is over," I whisper back.

Tatum flashes me a sympathetic smile. She knows exactly how Mom is and if I didn't have her with me for these meetings, I'm sure I would have to find more clever ways than a flat tire to get out of them.

As soon as the meeting is over, and the catering manager takes her ten-page packet of notes, front and back, with her, all attention turns to me.

"Olivia, have you found a date yet?" When I don't respond she continues, "I'll call Dr. Reinhart and see if his son is available. It's last minute, so I hope another woman hasn't snatched him up yet."

She digs in her purse for her phone, but I stop her with a hand on the table. "That's okay, Mom. I have a date." The lie curdles in my stomach. She pauses, her gaze meets mine, and all I can do is nod. Great. Now, I have to find a date. And right now, there's only one guy who comes to mind.

# CHAPTER FOURTEEN

# FML

*Olivia*

Once the meeting is over, I jump in my SUV with only one destination in my mind. I didn't want to resort to this, but I don't know what else to do. Pulling into his driveway, I park in front of the closed garage. In a few quick steps I'm up the sidewalk and knocking on his door.

Trey's frame fills the doorway, wearing jeans and a t-shirt, with his signature dazzling smile on full display. "Olivia? What are you doing here?"

"A couple things." I point a finger at him. "First, never call me sloppy seconds or trash ever again. In fact, never call any woman that."

"I'm sorry. No, you're right." He holds up three fingers tightly together. "I'll never use those words again."

"Good." My shoulders drop in relief. "Because second, I need your help."

"Anything. What do you need?" He leans his forearm on the doorjamb.

"I need a date for a charity event."

He drops his arm and crosses them over his chest. "And you're asking me? Don't you have a boyfriend for those kinds of things?"

I blow out a heavy breath. "I don't know what's going on with Ledger right now. Plus, I can't see him wanting to go to this kind of event."

"Did you decide this, or did he?"

"You know what? Never mind. Forget I asked." I twist around to leave, but he grips my wrist, stopping me.

"If you need a date, I'll do it. Tell me when and where." He gives me a half smile.

I wrap my arms around his neck in a tight hug. "Thank you so much. Seriously, you don't know how much this means to me."

"Anytime."

"So, meet me at my house on Saturday at five. There's a cocktail hour before dinner starts. You know the drill. Suit and tie, the whole works."

"I'll be there."

"Thank you. This means a lot." Excitedly, I clap my hands. "I'm off to buy a new dress. I'll talk to you later." One problem solved. Everything else will have to wait.

I put on a pair of sapphire earrings and take a step back. Hair is on point. Makeup is flawless. Dress is on fire. A small pang of guilt hits my stomach. Maybe I should have at least asked Ledger if he wanted to be my date? I'd just hate for him to be surrounded by people with their judgmental looks because he's a mechanic and doesn't wear a suit and tie everyday. No one should be subjected to that. So I'm actually doing him a favor. But also, we haven't spoken to each other all week.

A knock on my front door startles me. I glance at the time and it's 5 p.m. on the dot. I hustle down the stairs and open the door to greet Trey, only it's not Trey. Ledger stands before me in a dark gray Henley with the sleeves rolled up, ripped jeans and black combat boots. I swear somehow he got hotter in the past week. And I suddenly have the desire to climb him like a tree.

"Wow. You look …" his gaze wanders from my head to my bare feet and back up, "breathtaking."

"Ledger. What are you doing here?" I nervously tuck a loose strand of hair behind my ear, needing to busy myself.

"I wanted to come and apologize for everything that happened at my parents' house. I'm sorry. It became an awkward situation for everyone, especially for you in the middle. I know I should have said this earlier, but—"

I rest my hand on his arm. "It's not your fault. The situation is complicated, and no one knew that was going to happened."

"I know. I was hoping I could make it up to you, but by the way you're dressed, it looks like you already have plans tonight?"

This dress is too fancy for anything casual, so I'll go with the truth or half-truth. "I have this charity thing my mom puts on every year."

"Oh okay. You free tomorrow?"

His lips curve up into a half smile that instantly melt my panties. "Definitely. I would love that."

The rumble of a vehicle engine causes both of us to

turn around. A black Escalade pulls into my driveway behind my SUV.

*FML. This can't be happening.*

The car door opens and a shiny, black Oxford shoe hits the pavement, followed by another one. The door slams shut, and Trey removes his aviator sunglasses and hangs them on the collar of his pristine white button down.

Ledger's glare turns to me. "What's he doing here?" When I hesitate, he turns to Trey just as he strolls up the walkway to my house. "What are you doing here?" he asks Trey.

With a smug smile on his lips, he answers, "I'm her date."

"You're her date. To the charity event I knew nothing about. We don't talk for a week, and you replace me with him? I can't do this. I'm out." Ledger shoulders past Trey, almost knocking him down, and storms toward his truck parked in the driveway.

"Ledger! Wait! It's not what you think."

# CHAPTER FIFTEEN

## ALWAYS A BRIDESMAID

*Ledger*

Bare feet slap on the cement behind me, but I'm not in the mood for waiting. Before I can open the door to my truck, a warm, soft hand on my forearm stops me.

"Please, hear me out," she pleads.

I pull my arm away and her hand drops to her side. "Hear you out about what? That you asked another guy to be your date?" I sneer.

"It's not like that." Her shoulders deflate.

"Then tell me what it's like? Because the way I see it, the moment I'm out, you replaced me." I know I'm not being fair, but after what happened at my parents', she's quick to replace me with Trey.

"It's a fancy dinner that my mom hosts for charity. I didn't think it would be your thing."

"Why? Because I'm not good enough? Because I don't wear a tie every day? Because I don't make enough money? What is it?" My heartbeat roars in my ears. I've spent my entire life dealing with people looking down their noses at me, thinking they are better than me.

"It's none of that."

"Then what is it?" When she says nothing, I know my answer. "I can't do this. He's the type of guy you should be with." I point toward the house where Trey is standing. "Not me." I fling my door open, and she steps out of the way. The door slams as I sit and start the engine. I shift into reverse and back out of her driveway. Once I'm on the road, I step on the gas. My tires squealing as I speed away.

This situation shouldn't be this hard. But Trey always messes things up for me. All the way through high school, it was as if I was living in his shadow. He was the golden boy who got everything he wanted and didn't have to lift a finger to get it. While I had to bust my ass just to get by. I slam my palm against the steering wheel. Fuck! And once again, he wins. He's taking my girl on a date.

Since the dinner from hell at my parents' house, I've waged a war inside me. I've never met a girl like Olivia. Just her presence brightens my day, even on the shittiest of days. She's the brightest star in the darkest skies. And I've been a sad piece of shit this entire week without her. She's imprinted a piece of herself onto my soul, but she deserves better than me. Trey's right. I can't give her everything she deserves. After a few days of moping around the shop, as Jay would put it, he smacked some sense into me. He basically told me to man the fuck up. Don't let someone else dictate my life. Because at that moment, that's exactly what I was allowing Trey to do. Get in my head and wreak havoc once again. Showing up at her house today was the first step, but when Trey showed up, I couldn't handle it. Because he won. Just like he always does. And I'm tired of playing that game.

As I approach The Blue Anchor, I debate on stopping for a beer, but I think better of it. If I have one, I'm sure it will lead to two, three, and four and I might regret any decisions I make. Instead, I head home. At least if I drink my sorrows away alone, there won't be the possibility of waking up in someone else's bed.

I park my truck outside the closed garage door and make my way inside. On my way through the kitchen, I open the fridge and snag a beer. Twisting off the cap, I toss it into the garbage before strolling into the living room and throwing myself onto the couch. I'm starting to believe pathetic is my middle name. I slam the rest of my beer and get up to grab another, make that two. When I return to the living room, I find the remote, turn on the tv, and flip through the channels. Jack jumps up on the couch and curls his body next to mine. He bunts his head against my thigh, searching for attention, so I run my hand down his soft fur.

"You have it easy, Jack. Not a care in the world."

He stretches his legs as he gets comfortable, then shuts his one eye. Several hours later, I stir awake from a knock on my door.

*What time is it? And who the hell could be knocking?*

The knock sounds again, only louder this time. I stretch my limbs and Jack jumps off the couch and stretches himself. I rise to my feet, still drowsy from the nap and the beer. The knocking grows louder with each footfall. When I reach the door, I peek through the small window at the top and my chest tightens. Maybe I'm dreaming? Perhaps this entire day is a dream? I shake my head. Maybe I shouldn't have chugged those last two beers so fast. Twisting the doorknob, I pull it open. I blink once. Twice. "What are you doing here?"

## CHAPTER SIXTEEN

# YOU'RE MINE

*Olivia*

A tear pricks the corner of my eye as I watch his truck disappear down the road, then one on the other side, until they roll down my cheeks. I brush them away, hoping Trey doesn't notice.

"Everything okay?" Trey comes up behind me. His voice is soft, as if he's afraid to startle me.

"Yeah. Let me put my shoes on and we can go." I skirt past him, purposely avoiding eye contact. I don't want him to see me like this. Once inside, I touch up my makeup and hustle to strap on my heels. I bolt out the door, letting it slam behind me.

The Dashiell Ballroom is elegantly decorated with candles and low lighting. Circular tables fill the front of the ballroom close to the small stage while high tops fill the back half for those who want a more social atmosphere. That's exactly the purpose of these events. Everyone gets to brag about how much money they made last year, who bought the most expensive vacation property, and the gossip of who's sleeping with whom. All I can do is put on a fake smile and be supportive. That's what I've been told to do all my life.

"Olivia." My mom comes up to greet me with a kiss on both cheeks. Before she pulls away, she whispers, "The sapphire earrings? You should have gone with the diamonds." She turns to Trey. "And I see you brought a date."

I force a smile. "You remember Trey?"

Her eyes light up, but it's hard not to when Trey's large frame fills a three-thousand-dollar suit. "Yes. You're one of the head real estate agents at The Blue Stone Group."

"That's correct, Mrs. Ellis." Trey flashes her his most charming smile and she giggles. An actual teenage girl giggle. I roll my eyes.

"You can call me Tamara." She winks. "It's so wonderful you could join us. I'm sure you'll meet some potential clients here tonight. Ones that could really make your career skyrocket." She brushes her french manicured hand down the lapel of his suit jacket.

"I'm just here for Olivia," Trey says.

"Nonsense. These events are for socializing. One of the perks of dating my daughter. The Ellis name holds a lot of power in this city," she says.

Times like this make me wish no one knew my last name. That I was just another body in the crowd instead of using my last name as a perk for dating me.

"We're not dating. We're just friends." Trey wraps his arm around my shoulder and hugs me to him.

She whips her gaze to me. "Why not? Trey's an upstanding gentleman. You'd be lucky to be with a man like him."

"Mom," I grit between my teeth. "We are only friends."

"You should reconsider. You two would have the most adorable babies." She glances between the two of us.

Trey stifles a laugh while I roll my eyes. There's no stopping her, so I switch topics.

"Mom, have you seen Tatum?"

She glances around the ballroom. "Oh, she's around here somewhere."

"That's okay, we'll find her." I pull on Trey's arm, dragging him away from my mom.

Trey leans down so his mouth is next to my ear. "Did you hear that? We'd make adorable babies."

I backhand his stomach and he exhales an oomph. "Yeah. Not going to happen."

"Well how about we practice then?" He wiggles his eyebrows.

I shake my head with a laugh. "That's definitely not happening."

I spot Tatum standing at one of the high-top tables typing away on her phone. "Hey Tate! Am I glad to see you."

She fumbles to turn off her phone screen, and places it face down on the table.

"Hey, Olivia … and Trey?" She quirks an eyebrow at me.

I turn to Trey. "Can you get us some drinks?"

"Sure. What would you like?"

"Wine." I turn to Tatum. "Want anything?"

"Wine for me too. Thank you."

Trey saunters off. And I direct my attention to Tatum.

She tilts her head to the side, eyes trained on mine. "So, you're here with Trey?"

"Why is everyone surprised by that?" Kind of a dumb question to ask because what girl doesn't bring her boyfriend. At least I think he's still my boyfriend. Were we even boyfriend and girlfriend? I did meet the parents, so that must mean something even though it goes down in the record books as the worst meeting ever.

"Okay, but how does your boyfriend feel about you being on a date with another man, most importantly his brother?" She tilts her head at me. I had no idea I would end up being the evening's gossip topic.

"Half-brother. But that's a completely different story. Ledger showed up at my house today, right before Trey arrived."

She shifts to face me, concern etched on her face. "What happened?"

"He was upset that Trey showed up to be my date. I don't know what to do. He's said nothing to me all week, and then when he does, I'm with Trey. I don't know if things can get any messier at this point. Plus, this is more Trey's style. Ledger wouldn't fit in here." I glance behind me, and Trey is chatting with an older investment banker. "See. Trey's in his element. I can't picture Ledger talking to these people. And what would he talk about? How to replace an engine. The people here don't care about that. They just take it somewhere to have it done for them."

"People like Ledger?" She raises an eyebrow.

"Yes. No. Not like that. This just isn't his style."

She shrugs. "I hope he was the one to make that decision."

Why does everyone keep saying that? Instead of answering her, I divert the attention back to her. "Where's Adam?"

"Oh. He couldn't make it." She flings her hand in the air as if she's brushing her words away. "Got caught up with something at work, but he made a donation in his absence."

"I'm sorry Tate." I rest my hand on hers.

"It's fine."

Trey returns to our table with our drinks. Before he can set mine down, I'm stealing it from his grip and taking a giant gulp. There's a slight chance I'm going to need several of these to get through the night.

The entire time through dinner, I pick at my food. Eating a bite here and there. My mind on Ledger. Maybe I made a mistake about not asking him to come? I know I would have had a lot more fun with him here. By the time dessert arrives, I'm not even eating. I'm just pushing the dulce de leche cheesecake around on my plate while everyone talks amongst themselves. I'm listening enough to nod and smile at the appropriate times, but otherwise their conversation is like white noise.

Trey leans over. "I'm surprised you made it the entire meal."

"What do you mean?" I whisper.

"Olivia, I know you. There hasn't been a genuine smile on your face since we got here. I'm surprised you haven't ditched this place to go find Ledger."

"I won't leave you here to fend for yourself."

"Seriously, you don't need to worry about me. I've already scored one potential deal. I'm going to work the crowd again after dinner to see what else I can get. By then, they'll be a few scotches deep and might be more willing to write some checks. Go make up with Ledger." He nudges my arm.

I narrow my eyes at him. "Why are you suddenly team Ledger?"

"Look, I don't want to get into it here. We have a long and complicated relationship. I see how much you like him, and I want you to be happy."

I give him a half smile. "He was pretty mad. What do I do if he was telling the truth and he's really done?"

He drops his chin and looks me square in the eyes. "Where's the don't take no for an answer Olivia I'm used to? Make him hear you out and don't take no for an answer."

"Are you sure I should go see him?"

"Yes, unless you're stalling because you want to stay here so we can try that kiss again." The corner of his lips tip up into a smile.

A small laugh escapes me, and I shake my head. "Good try."

"I take my shots when I can." He shrugs. "Want me to give you a ride?"

"No, I'll Uber. But also, do you have his address?"

"You don't know where he lives?"

"No. We've always gone to my house or his shop." He rattles off Ledger's address, and I type it into my phone. "And if my mom comes looking for me, make something up?"

"Moms love me. I'll come up with something good."

"I'm kind of afraid of that. Thanks Trey." Leaning over, I place a kiss on his cheek. Then I toss my napkin on my plate and push my chair out to stand. My gaze wanders around the room until I find my parents busy talking with another senator and his wife. Now's my chance. I slink along the rear wall of the ballroom and once I know no one is watching, I'm out the front entrance.

I rush past the windows, ducking behind bushes to make sure I'm not caught. When the coast is clear, I pull out my phone from my purse and open the Uber app. I type in Ledger's address, hoping he's at home and not at the shop or, even worse, with someone else.

The Uber pulls up to the curb of the ballroom and I hop in. It's a twenty-minute drive across town to Ledger's house. My leg bounces on the floorboard of the Uber. I don't know what his reaction will be when I show up unannounced. Maybe he is done with me, and this is just a sorry attempt for nothing. Every possible scenario flits through my mind. And each one makes me more and more anxious.

The Uber pulls up at the curb in front of his house. A light in the living room glows through the window. I pause a moment with my hand on the door handle. The driver turns around and asks, "Do you want me to wait?"

"No. That's okay. Thank you."

I get out and close the door behind me. Lifting the front of my dress, I climb the stairs that lead up to the front door, careful to avoid getting my heel stuck in one of the cracks in the cement. I blow out a breath. Here goes nothing. With my hand raised, I knock on the door. A few seconds pass and there's no answer. So, I knock a little harder. My heartbeat pounds in my chest. What if he's purposely ignoring me? What if he really done with me? My knock still goes unanswered, so I try one last time.

The door flies open, and a wide-eyed Ledger greets me. "What are you doing here?"

"I'm sorry. I should have never assumed you didn't want to go. I should have asked you and let you make that decision instead of me making it for you. But also, you don't get to walk away."

"So, you left your party to tell me that?"

I nod. "I'm here to fight for this. Whatever this is." I

pause. My gaze scans his face. His expression gives nothing away. His indifference breaks my heart into tiny pieces, but I'm determined to not give up, so I try one last time. "Going with Trey meant nothing. We're only friends. You're the one I want to be with. I want you. And I hope you still want me too."

He reaches forward, his eyes darken from steely gray to almost black as he wraps a hand around the nape of my neck, hauling me to him. His fingertips dig into my skin, and he slams his lips to mine. He twists us around, walking me backward into the house. He kicks the door shut with his heel and pushes me against the nearest wall, all the while never breaking our kiss. I moan as I bring my hands up to rest on his chest.

With his palm pressing against the wall next to my head, he pulls away. My lips follow his, wanting more. Needing more. But he rests his forehead against mine and whispers, "You realize I'm no good for you."

I lift my chin. "You're exactly what I need."

He pushes off the wall, taking a step back. "Just look at you. You're wearing a dress that costs more than my mortgage, don't get me wrong, you look fucking gorgeous and," he holds out his arms, "I'm in jeans with grease stains and a worn shirt. We don't belong together. I'm the guy you take your car to when you need it fixed. Not the one you take to your fancy parties."

"But you're the only one who makes me feel alive. Your kiss makes me go lightheaded. Your touch sends goosebumps all over my body. But mostly I can't stop thinking about you and wanting to be near you." I inch closer to him. "I made a mistake tonight and I won't do it again. I don't care about any of this." Bunching the skirt of my dress in my hands, I lift the fabric and it drops to the floor. "In fact ..." I raise my arm where the zipper is and tug it down. Once the dress is loose, I let it fall to my feet. I step over the pile of fabric and closer to him. Standing in his entryway, I'm only wearing a black, strapless lace bustier, matching black thong, and garter.

He stares at me, taking me in. I won't lie. I love the way he admires me, like I'm the only person in the entire world. My chest rises and falls from his heated gaze.

"You come here to tempt me?" he grits out.

"Is it working?"

He charges me, pushing me until my back smashes against the door. His long, thick fingers wrap around my throat, holding me in place. His fingers squeeze my neck. Not too tight, but tight enough to know he's there. "What do you not understand? I'm not good for you," he seethes. "I'm not the one you should be with. I don't want you."

I inhale a sharp breath and my nostrils flare. "I call bullshit. A man wouldn't kiss me the way you did if he didn't want me."

"And you think you can get whatever you want?" He tilts his head, his lips are inches from mine.

"I don't think. I know I can have you."

"Is that so?"

"Yes." I lift my chin, holding my head high. I'm not leaving here unless he physically removes me. I know he wants this too. His words may say one thing, but the lust and desire swirling in his irises says otherwise.

"Just know there's no turning back."

"Good."

He releases his grip and trails a finger from the column of my neck, down to the valley between my breasts.

The tip of his nose brushes against mine. "Being with me isn't easy."

My gaze meets his. "I don't want easy."

He glances down at my lips and then meets my eyes. His voice is deep and growly. "We do this, you're mine."

"Say it again," I whisper.

"You're mine."

# CHAPTER SEVENTEEN

## GREEDY GIRL

*Olivia*

Now it's my turn to attack him. I jump into his arms and wrap my legs around his waist. His hands cup my ass to keep me from falling. I press my palms to his cheeks and kiss him with fervor.

"You're so fucking beautiful, duchess. Let me show you just how bad I can be." His fingers dig into the soft flesh of my butt. Every squeeze and flex of his fingers sends a delicious tingle through my body. I know what his strong hands are capable of, and I want them touching me … everywhere. His mouth moves to my cheek, pressing kisses there. The stubble on his face brushing against my sensitive skin has me reminiscing about the last time he was between my legs. My arousal soaks my panties just thinking about it. He trails kisses down to my neck. He bites down then sucks on the same spot.

"Ahh! That feels so good." I moan. "You'll be my bad boy and I'll be your good girl." I flinch and pinch my eyes shut. "Oh my God. That was cheesy, wasn't it?"

He chuckles then presses his lips to mine. "No. It was cute. But know when I'm through with you, you'll be bad, too."

"Yes! Do all the bad things to me. I'm yours." Another moan escapes me as he continues to kiss and nip on my sensitive skin.

Effortlessly, he carries me in his arms a few feet into the living room. When we're at the side of the couch, he releases me. I slide down his body, every dip and valley of his hard chest runs along my fingertips, stopping when his now rock hard cock presses into my stomach.

He takes a step back. "You won't be needing this."

The elastic snaps as he releases the strap connected to my stockings. His hand skims around my waist and over the curve of my ass as he undoes those straps as well. Then his hand skates up my back and unclasps my black lace bustier. The fabric loosens as each hook releases from the eyelet. My chest heaves in anticipation. After several agonizing seconds it falls to the floor at my feet. My heavy breasts jiggle. The cold air mixing with my arousal causes my nipples to pebble to stiff peaks. Ledger takes that as an invitation. His hand cups one heavy breast while his mouth descends on the other. In tandem he circles this tongue around one nipple while doing the same with this thumb on the other. He bites down on the stiff peak and pinches the other, sending a jolt of electricity straight to my core. White hot heat blasts through me from the dual sensation and I can't help the moan that falls from my lips.

"I love how responsive your body is to my touch. It

makes me want to see what else I can do." His warm breath skates across my heated skin.

"Yes. I want it. All of it." I arch my back, pressing my breasts farther into him.

"Are you sure you can take it?" He bites down on the soft skin on the side of my breast.

"Yes," I moan.

With a grip on my shoulders, he turns me around. "Bend over. Palms on the armrest."

My heart hammers in my chest as I do what he says. I've never had a guy be so demanding before and I love it. It's thrilling and turns me on more than I ever thought possible, or maybe it's just Ledger.

"I love your flawless, creamy skin, but it will look even better if I add some color. Have you ever been spanked?"

I peer over my shoulder. My teeth dig into my bottom lip as I shake my head. A thrill shoots through me. Being with Ledger is more than a relationship, it's an experience. And I want everything.

"You really are a good girl. If it's too much tell me." His breath against the shell of my ear sends a tingle through my body. He may be rough and demanding, but he's also sweet and caring wanting to make sure I'm comfortable.

A second later, there's a loud crack immediately followed by a sharp sting as his palm strikes my butt cheek. I gasp and then moan when he massages the spot and places a kiss on my shoulder. But the moment doesn't last long before he does it again, sending a delicious sting coursing through my body.

"You like that duchess? Want me to keep going?" he whispers in my ear.

"Yes." I'm seconds away from begging.

Another smack sounds through the room, followed by

my moans while he massages my tender flesh. The pain mixed with the pleasure is a sensation I've never felt before. I know it's one I'll want more of. All my past boyfriends have always handled me like a delicate flower, but not Ledger. And I want all of it.

"How wet are you for me?"

"Soaked."

He trails a finger down my ass crack but stops at my puckered hole. "Has anyone been inside you here?" He presses a finger to the tight muscle through the strap of my thong.

"No," I choke out.

He circles the area, applying slight pressure in between rotations. I can't help pushing back against him, getting more turned on from the feeling.

"I think my good girl wants my cock to be the first." I moan again as he adds more pressure. "But not tonight. I have other plans for you."

I release a faint whimper when he moves his hand and travels farther down until he's between my legs. He runs his finger over the thin fabric covering my pussy and circles my clit.

"You're dripping for me." He pushes my panties to the side and runs a finger up my slit.

"I need you, Ledger." I push against him, encouraging him to continue.

He shoves a finger inside me, and my body jerks forward when his knuckles push against me. My moans and whimpers grow louder with each thrust. He pulls out and spears me with two fingers this time.

"Oh! Yes! That feels so good." I wiggle my ass, wanting more of him.

He continues to plunge his fingers in and out of me as

he whispers in my ear. "No more talking. You going to take my dick like a good girl?"

The tips of his fingers curl into me, hitting my g-spot. "Yes!" I cry out. He pulls out of me and I whimper at the loss.

"Greedy girl. But don't worry, soon I'll be filling you with my cock."

Glancing over my shoulder, my gaze is fixated on his strong hands as he flicks open the button on his jeans. My chest heaves as I wait in anticipation. A shiver courses through me when the cold metal ball at the tip of his head runs down my slit. I push against him, needing him inside me. He continues to rub the head up and down, coating himself in my arousal. My fingers dig into the arm of the couch, not wanting to wait any longer. He lines up with my entrance and slowly pushes the head in.

"Oh Ledger!" My neck arches as he continues to inch inside me, stretching me twice as much as his fingers did. The metal balls rub against my inner walls, creating an all-new sensation that I've never experienced before. Once he's fully inside me, he stills.

"Your pussy is gripping me so tight. I'm afraid to move."

I take matters into my own hands and rock against him. He releases a deep groan, but I continue picking up the pace with longer and faster strokes. Ledger takes over, driving deep inside me. Each thrust harder than the last. My nails dig into the armrest. My moans mix with his grunts. He reaches around with one arm wrapped around my chest while his other hand rubs my clit. With my back arched, his piercing hits me in the right spot on every thrust. He pinches my nipple, and that's my undoing. I cry out in pleasure as my orgasm rips through me like a tsunami. But

Ledger relentlessly continues pounding into me, chasing his own release. Wave after wave of pleasure crash into me as a second orgasm takes over. My legs tremble and if Ledger wasn't holding me up, I'm sure I'd crash to the floor. With one last thrust, Ledger roars out his release. His heavy breathing slows as he drops his arm to my waist and presses lazy kisses to my shoulder. A moment later, he stops.

"Fuck." His chest is pressed against me, his breathing labored.

"Fuck is right. I'm pretty sure I blacked out for a moment."

"No. I mean, I don't think I've ever come that hard. But I'm not wearing a condom."

My body tenses. "Oh." I pause. "I'm on birth control. And I get tested regularly. Everything's negative."

His warm lips press to my shoulder again, and he pulls out. "Same. Well, I'm not on birth control, but I got tested recently, and it's negative."

I chuckle. "So, we're good?"

"More than good. Hold on. Let me clean you up." I glance over my shoulder, and he disappears around the corner. He returns with a warm washcloth for me. When he's finished, he tugs on his boxer briefs, and he holds out his t-shirt for me. I lift my arms and he tugs it over my head.

"Stay the night with me?"

"Sex and a sleepover. How can a girl say no to that?"

He tugs me to him and buries his face in the crook of my neck. "Mostly, I'm tired and don't want to take you home right now."

I laugh. "You should have stopped at stay the night with me."

He bends at the knees and lifts me up. I squeal in surprise as I wrap my legs around his waist. He carries me through the house until we reach his bedroom. Without turning on the light, he tosses me onto the bed, then he joins me. He grabs the bottom corner of the comforter and throws it over both of us. I snuggle into his chest as he wraps an arm around me. As soon as his head hits the pillow, his breathing evens out until he's softly snoring. I've never experienced sex like that. It was wild, animalistic, and I'm sure I'll be sore tomorrow. But it was worth it and I can't wait to do it again and again. My lips pull into a smile as I drift off into a peaceful, orgasm induced sleep.

I stir awake to a heavy arm draped across my waist from behind. My eyes flutter open and my breath hitches. Reaching around me, I tap Ledger's hip.

"Hmm." He nuzzles his nose into my hair at my neck as he pulls me closer to him.

"Ledger?"

"Yeah." His voice is gravelly from sleep.

"Please tell me you have a one-eyed cat who sits on your dresser and stares at you while you sleep."

Ledger lifts his head and peers over my shoulder. "Oh yeah. That's Jack. If it looks like he's judging you, it's probably because he is."

My gaze wanders to Jack, who still hasn't blinked. Remind me to never have a staring contest with him. "Did you give your cat a human name as a funny play on words? That way when your friends ask you if you want to hang out, but you don't want to, you can tell them, 'I can't.. I'm hanging out with Jack tonight'. Then they don't think you're boring when you're actually at home sitting on your couch with your cat."

His chest rumbles behind me. "No. But I might have to

use that sometime. His full name is Captain Jack Sparrow. Jack for short."

"Ah, since he has one eye. I get it. Also, how did he lose his eye?" I roll over to face Ledger.

"I found him behind the dumpster at the shop. He looked pretty rough, like he got in a fight with a rival cat gang and lost some street cred. I took him to the vet. They said they could save him, but they'd have to remove his injured eye and neuter him. At that point, I felt bad he was losing an eye and his nuts on the same day, so, the least I could do was give him a home."

Jack must know we're talking about him since he jumps off the dresser and onto the end of the bed. He saunters his way up the middle and cuddles next to Ledger.

"That's the sweetest thing ever. The bad boy and his cat." I pet Jack's head and he purrs.

We had an amazing night last night, but I'm still left with more questions than answers about Ledger. Might as well rip off the band-aid. I turn my head on the pillow so I'm looking at him. "So, what's the full story between you and Trey?"

He rolls to his back, the tension in the room building like a summer thunderstorm. Even Jack notices and jumps off the bed. His back claws scrape on the hardwood floor as he scurries away.

"It's long and complicated."

I inch closer to him. "I'm here to listen. Plus, I want to get to know you more."

He sits up, resting against the wall, his gaze trained on the ceiling. He inhales a deep breath and slowly releases it. "You already know we share the same dad, different moms."

I sit up, wrapping a blanket around me and crossing my legs like a pretzel, giving him my undivided attention.

He continues. "Might as well start from the beginning. Our dad and my mom met at a party after college graduation. Mom wasn't a student but was at the party. They had a one-night stand, they went their separate ways, and Mom found out she was pregnant. She spent years hunting for him, but every lead turned into a dead end, and it was taking a toll on her. Growing up, we didn't have a lot of money, but we scraped by."

Without saying a word, I rest my hand on his forearm. I want him to know I'm here for him. He glances down, the corner of his mouth twitches into a slight smile.

"When I was around five years old, she found him. But she was devastated to learn he got married and had a kid." He blows out a long breath before continuing. "She confronted him. Had a DNA test done. He offered support financially, but that's when my mom spiraled out of control." I brush my thumb across his arm, encouraging him to continue. "From then until I was about fifteen, she got into drugs and made poor decisions in the guys she dated. She stopped being a mom, and essentially, I raised myself. I did what I wanted, when I wanted. Eventually, she found herself in the back of a cop car and behind bars for trafficking methamphetamine."

"I'm so sorry, Ledger. That must have been so hard."

He nods. "After that, they forced me to move into my dad's house. Punk kid moving from the bad neighborhood to the one with mansions and swimming pools." He huffs out a humorless laugh. "It was a recipe for disaster."

Tilting my head, I ask, "How so?"

"I tried to be on my best behavior, but have you ever tried to tame a wild animal? It only lasts for so long before all hell breaks loose. And that was me. I never had to live with rules and suddenly I'm being told where I needed to be, how I needed to dress, what time to be home. It wasn't what I was accustomed to. Trey and I are close in age. I'm a year older than him, so throughout high school it felt like a competition. He was the good kid that everyone loved. All he had to do was skate by. And I was the young punk that had to bust my ass to get noticed. Obviously, we ran in different crowds so that fueled our hatred for each other. Then girls got involved." He glances up toward the ceiling and huffs out a small laugh. "It's like they all wanted bragging rights that they were with two brothers. One would date Trey and then me or vice versa. It basically became a pissing match that drove an even bigger wedge between us. But then I met Archie, and he kicked my ass into shape."

I scoot closer to him. I love that he's opening up to me and I want to know everything about him. "How did he do that?"

"One night I was out with some friends, and we broke into a mechanic shop to steal some tools to pawn. I can't remember how, but we got caught. Well, I got caught. My friends ran away. That's when I met Archie. He said he wouldn't press charges, but I had to work off the damage we did. I remember he told me," his voice lowers, "'If you don't show up for work, I'll hunt you down.' He never finished that sentence, and I didn't want to find out what he'd do if he had to hunt me down, so every day I made sure I was five minutes early." He laughs at the memory. "Archie saved my life that day. He took me under his wing and put me to work. He helped me build my business to what it is today."

I scoot closer to him. "Wow. That story is just … wow." I pause, unsure of what to say. "Archie sounds like an incredible man."

"He is. He's a hardass, but he saw something in me. He

knew exactly how to motivate me to stop being a punk and grow up. You'll have to meet him someday."

"I would like that." I shift to sit next to him, loop my arms with his, and rest my head on his shoulder.

"Me too."

# CHAPTER EIGHTEEN

# UNWELCOME SURPRISE

## Ledger

As each day passes with no sign of Stevie, I wonder if she'll show up at all. I just hope she's okay. A part of me will always care for her, but we're not good for each other. Too bad it took years of arguments to figure that out. While I wasn't looking for marriage and kids, I wanted to settle my life down and grow some roots, mainly with my shop. Stevie has always been a free spirit, going wherever the wind blows. While it was fun for a while, I didn't want that anymore. The last time she took off when I wanted to stay was the last straw. When she returned and found my house locked, she realized it was finally over. We've seen each other sparingly over the years and a few times have jumped back into bed after a few too many shots of whiskey, but it's never been the same. It never will be.

I ratchet in a spark plug in my 1980s Harley Davidson Shovelhead. For the past five months, I've spent my spare time restoring and rebuilding the engine and it's finally time to test it out. The frame sits on a jack stand. It's all bare bones except for the engine, gas tank, and rear tire. I stand and grab the gas can and pour a little into the tank.

"Are you finally going to fire her up?" Jay walks into the shop and stands beside me.

"Yep."

He rubs his hands together. "I can't wait to listen to her purr."

I turn the key and press the electric start. It sputters a little but doesn't start. I pull the choke lever to give it a little more gas and try again. This time, she rumbles to life. I rev the engine, the roar echoing off the walls in the shop.

"Hell yeah!" Jay shouts over the noise.

A small smile plays on my lips. After five months, I was able to make her rise from the dead. Granted, I still have a lot more work to do with the body, but the heart and soul of the machine is alive.

Jay clasps me on the shoulder. "This bike is going to be so bad ass once you get it on the street. I'm glad I was here to witness the first start."

"Thanks, man. Me too." It's times like this that I live for. When all the blood, sweat, and tears finally come to fruition.

"I better go work on this AC clutch. It's being a real bitch."

"Since I'm done with this, I'll come help you." I kill the engine.

A couple hours later, I've finished helping Jay, and I take a seat in my office. I scan my calendar for the week and make sure I have all the parts I need. My phone vibrates on my desk. When I glance down, Olivia's name pops up on the screen.

"Hey, duchess."

"Hey, yourself. What are you doing right now?"

Hearing her voice sends all the blood rushing south. I adjust myself in my work pants. "Thinking of you."

"You're so full of it."

"No lie. You can come to the shop right now and I'll show you."

She laughs. The sound is sweet and innocent. But I know she is far from innocent, though there are a few things I'm sure I could still teach her.

"How about you come over tonight? I'll get some takeout. And then I can show you what was delivered today. Spoiler alert. There's lots of sheer fabric and lace."

I adjust myself again. "Mmm. I can picture it now. Right before I rip it off your body."

"Maybe this time you can admire it a little longer than five minutes before it becomes scrap fabric. Expensive scrap fabric."

"Don't buy it and then I won't have to tear it off your sexy as hell body."

"Sadly, that's the fun part."

*Bang. Bang. Bang.*

"Hey Ledger! You should come out here. We got a problem," Jay yells from the other side of my closed office door.

I roll my eyes and cover the phone. "You're a big boy! Figure it out!"

A second passes without a reply and I think he may have solved his own problem. "No. This is a problem only you can fix."

"Son of a bitch," I mutter under my breath. "Give me a minute!"

"Hey duchess. I gotta go. Apparently, I only hire incompetent mechanics."

"No problem. I'll see you tonight?"

"Fuck yeah. And you better be wearing that sheer fabric thing when you answer the door."

She laughs again. "I'll see what I can do."

I press end and set my phone down on my desk. I exhale a huff and scrub my hands down my face. Pushing away from my desk, I exit the office. My feet carry me down the hallway until I reach the open part of the garage. Two of my part-time mechanics stand off to the left. One is leaning against the tool bench running a rag over a car part while another one stands next to him. My eyebrows knit together as both stare me down, a small smirk on both their faces.

I revert my gaze to the right where Jay is standing. "Now what the fuck couldn't you handle by yourself?"

Jay steps out of the way.

An all too familiar face, with long raven hair, steps out from behind one of the parked cars in the garage. "Hi Ledge."

## CHAPTER NINETEEN

# FML PART TWO

## *Ledger*

My entire body tenses. Time ceases to exist. The one person I never expected to see is standing in my shop. And she looks the same as she did all those years ago.

"Are you just going to stand there or are you going to say hi?"

I crash down to Earth with a heavy thud. There's extra sass in her voice. One I'm all too familiar with.

"What are you doing here, Stevie?" My voice is stern. I shouldn't be surprised to see her here, yet I'm surprised to see her here.

"Really? After all these years, this is how you're going to greet me?" She sashays toward me. Her knee-high black boots clack against the cement. She holds her arms out toward me. Before we're toe to toe, I sidestep her. "I guess it is going to be like that." She crosses her arms over her chest and pops her hip.

"I'm not going to ask again, Stevie. Why are you here?" I cross my arms over my chest, mimicking her pose.

"I wanted to see you." She softens her voice, but I'm not buying it.

"Are you fucking kidding me? I haven't seen you in five years and even then, it was more of a passing nod. Then you just show up at my shop, expecting a welcome home party?" I grit through my teeth.

"You know what? Clearly, I'm not wanted here, so I'll go." She spins around and stomps toward the open overhead garage door.

I lift my face toward the ceiling. If I knew what was good for me, I'd let her walk out of here, but I can't. For Archie. I blow out an exasperated huff. "Wait." Stevie stops in her tracks, almost as if she was waiting for me to say something.

Slowly, she twists around to face me. The slight crinkle in her eye gives her away. Son of a bitch. She played me.

"Be straight with me. Why are you here?"

She saunters the few steps until she's standing in front of me. "I need to be somewhere that feels like home."

"So why didn't you go see your dad?"

"Because I wanted to see you." She takes a step closer and drags a finger down the front of my shirt.

I clasp her wrist, stopping her progress. "Not happening." Her bottom lip juts out. I drop her wrist and her arm falls to her side. "I'm going to call Archie. Let him know where you are."

"No need. I called him before I got here. It will be a few days before he's back. Who knew he'd send out a search party for me?" She shrugs.

My blood boils from her nonchalance. I take a step

closer to her, my face inches from her, and I spit out, "Do you think of anyone besides yourself?"

She bats her eyelashes. "I thought about you. That's why I'm here."

All I can do is snarl my lip and shake my head. "I'm calling Archie and letting him know myself. Don't move." Without waiting for any response, I stomp to the other side of the garage. Jay and another mechanic, Mike, are staring at me as I pass. I glare at them, and they scurry to busy themselves as if they weren't watching the shit show that just went down.

When I reach my office, I kick my door shut and pull out my phone. Quickly, I dial Archie and, sure enough, he confirms Stevie talked to him and he'll come pick her up in a few days. Then he asked me to watch over her until he returns. Of course, I told him I would. But she's a grown woman. She shouldn't need babysitting.

After I hang up with Archie, I make my way to the garage. Stevie's still standing where I left her, swirling a strand of her sleek, midnight black locks around her finger as she pouts her lips. It's the same look she would flash me all those years ago that would have me ravishing her body in seconds. Now ... nothing.

"Archie confirmed your story."

"Did you think I was lying?"

I narrow my eyes at her.

"Okay. Okay. That's all in the past." She prowls toward me. "So, am I staying at your place while I wait for my dad?"

Fuck. She's going to need a place to stay. I don't trust her at my house, but I need her close to keep an eye on her.

"You can stay in the garage."

She glances around the shop and her lip curls. "Really? The garage? Am I some sort of dog or something?"

"There's a makeshift bedroom with a fully functioning bathroom." Years ago, when I first got the shop, I didn't have any extra money, so I lived here, which included setting up a makeshift bedroom. If this were any other time, I would invite her to my place but, fuck. Archie would kick my ass if I made his daughter stay in the garage. I hope I'm not going to regret this. "Fine. You can stay at my place. Grab your bags and throw them in my truck."

Her lips turn up in a slow smile.

*I'm going to regret this.*

Stevie grabs her bags and saunters toward my truck. A low whistle sounds next to me. When I glance over, Jay's at my side.

"You're really letting her stay at your place?"

"As much as I want to, I can't kick her out to the street."

"Well, good luck resisting that one while she's sleeping in your bed, probably wearing some skimpy, lacy thing on your sheets."

I narrow my eyes at him. He holds his hands up in defense and slowly reverses his steps, but the devilish smile never leaves his face. It will only be for a few days. No one will know and then my life can go back to normal.

"Are you ready?" Stevie yells from the open garage door.

I turn to Jay. "I'll be back. Get some shit done around here while I'm gone."

"So, while I'm working here, you'll be working her?"

I glare at Jay. My fists clench. I'm three seconds away from physically assaulting my friend, but instead I take the high road. For this, he'll be scraping and polishing the head gaskets for the car we're fixing later. I walk to the open garage door and past Stevie until I'm pulling open the door to my truck. With the key in the ignition, she jumps in as the truck rumbles to life.

Fifteen minutes later, we're pulling into the driveway of my duplex. My place isn't the swankiest place in town, but it's mine. It was the first thing I purchased once I got my shop up and running. Jay rents out the top half since I don't need an entire house to myself. The truck door slams behind me, and I stroll up to the door at ground level. When I glance behind me, Stevie is carting two suitcases down the uneven sidewalk.

"Don't worry. I got everything." She huffs as she hoists a suitcase up onto the cement landing.

"I never doubted you."

She tilts her head and narrows her eyes.

I unlock the door and push it open, holding it open for her to walk in.

"Now you're a gentleman."

"Never claimed to be one."

"Oh, I know. I remember all the times when you had me pinned up against the wall—"

"Stevie, I'm not doing this. No walks down memory lane." I yank the suitcases from her and lead her through the small kitchen, into the living room, and around the corner to my bedroom. The suitcases hit the floor with a plop. "I'm only doing this for Archie."

I toss a pillow to the floor. Then I strip the blanket and sheets off the bed and toss the sheet ball into the corner of the room. I pull open the closet door and grab a set of clean sheets and pillowcases from the top shelf. While Stevie stares from the other side of the room, I fold the fitted sheet over the last corner of the mattress and toss the sheet on top, along with the comforter.

"I'm sure you can finish the rest." I grab the pillow off the floor and pull a blanket from the closet before closing the door.

"Where are you going?" she asks as her footsteps trail behind me.

"I'll be sleeping on the couch."

"We're adults. We can share a bed. It will be like the good old days." She tosses me a wink.

"That's not happening."

"Why not? Remember those nights where we would stay up past sun rise and not talk? You don't want to relive those nights again, or do you have a girlfriend?" I freeze at the last word. "Oh. You have a girlfriend. How's she going to react when she finds out your ex-girlfriend is sleeping in your bed?"

"She won't. Because she's not going to find out. And she's not my girlfriend." I don't need Stevie knowing about Olivia. If Stevie came with a warning, it would be 'doesn't play well with other females.' Keeping these two far away from each other is the best thing for all parties involved.

"With that reaction, she's something. And if you think she won't find out … you're denser than a box of rocks."

"You're only here for a day, two max. Then I'll continue with my life."

"Oh, this should be good." She plops down on the couch and kicks her feet up on the coffee table. "So, what are we doing today?"

"I'm going back to the garage. You're going to stay right here."

"Wait." She jumps to her feet. "You're leaving. And you're banishing me to your place like a child."

"Don't act like one and I won't treat you like one." I snag my truck keys from the table in the kitchen. Stevie's footsteps follow me from the living room.

"Wow. Okay. I'll just sit here until you get back then."

"Finally. You're listening for once." I storm out the door, letting it slam behind me.

When I arrive at the shop, Jay and I finish installing the new AC clutch. As I'm washing my hands, my phone vibrates in my pocket. Quickly, I dry my hands and pull out my phone.

A text from Olivia pops up.

OLIVIA

What kind of takeout did you want? I was debating between Indian and Chinese.

Fuck. I've been so preoccupied since Stevie showed up and getting this car finished, I forgot about our plans tonight. I can't leave Stevie alone all night.

I type out a quick reply.

LEDGER

Sorry, something came up. Rain check?

OLIVIA

What could be more important than me, you, and a silk corset from La Perla?

I groan. I don't know what La Perla is, but I'm familiar with the everything else. And fuck, I want to see that. I want to tell her nothing and that I'll be over right now. But I can't.

LEDGER

As much as I want that threesome, a buddy needs my help. How about I take you for a motorcycle ride this weekend to make up for it?

OLIVIA

*Thinking Emoji* It's a good start.

LEDGER

I could fuck that pretty pussy of yours while I bend you over my motorcycle.

OLIVIA

You're getting warmer.

LEDGER

Have you scream my name while I pound into you.

OLIVIA

Hotter

LEDGER

I'll stroke your clit until you cum all over my cock.

OLIVIA

Ding! Ding! Ding!

LEDGER

I'll talk to you later.

Fuck. Now I'm rock hard, and I have to go home where Stevie is. I better wait this one out for a bit.

## CHAPTER TWENTY

# BAD ASS PRINCE CHARMING

## *Ledger*

It's been a day and a half and still no word from Archie yet. I hoped he'd be here by now. Because with each passing day, it's getting harder and harder to keep this shit a secret. I stretch my legs and they meet the arm of the couch. I can't even stretch properly. Also, sleeping on the couch sucks. Couches aren't meant for sleeping. Beds are made for sleeping. Currently, mine is housing an unwanted guest. The blanket slides off me and hits the floor. A small gasp catches my attention and my eyes pop open.

"Good morning, Ledge."

I rub the sleep from my eyes as they adjust to the bright sunlight shining in through the curtainless window.

*Note to self: get some fucking curtains.*

Stevie sits on the edge of the coffee table in front of

138

me, one leg crossed over the other, wearing only a t-shirt. In fact, one of my t-shirts.

"Why are you wearing my shirt? And why are you staring at me?" I glare at her.

She leans closer, resting her elbows on her knee. "I always loved wearing your shirts to bed."

I roll my eyes. "Doesn't give you free rein to them now."

"You want it back?" She smirks as she grips the hem of the shirt and lifts.

Hurriedly, I tug on her wrist, preventing her from lifting the shirt any farther. "Keep it. It's yours now. Back to my other question, why are you staring at me?"

"I woke up to your cat staring at me, so I thought that's what you do in this house. And when did you get a cat?"

"Months ago."

She tilts her head, studying me. "You never seemed like a cat person. Let alone getting one so mean. It hissed at me."

I want to tell her that's because Jack can sense bad people, but that's a discussion I don't have time for. "A lot has changed. There are many things you don't know about me."

"Maybe we should rectify that." Her gaze wanders over my body and stops at my dick tenting my boxer briefs. I reach for the blanket on the floor and cover myself.

"I've always loved your tattoos. I see you've gotten a few new ones since the last time I saw you. Including the one that runs down your torso and disappears under the waistband. I'd love to see where it ends." Her tongue peeks out, wetting her bottom lip.

"Yeah, that's not going to happen." I move to sit up while keeping the blanket at my waist. "New rule. No more watching me sleep. You already have my bedroom. What more do you want?"

Her gaze drops to my lips, then up to meet mine. "You."

She rises to her feet in front of me. The hem of the shirt kisses the tops of her thighs. She inches closer before resting one knee on the couch and then the other until she's straddling me. Her palm lies flat against my chest and pushes me until I hit the back of the couch. It all happens so quick, I don't realize what she's doing until she's on my lap.

"You don't have to do anything. Just sit there and I'll do all the work." She trails a finger over my cheek and across my jaw.

"Stevie." My voice is low and deep.

"No one has to know," she whispers as she runs her nose along mine.

"Stevie." My voice is more stern this time.

"I promise." Her lips move an inch closer to mine.

"Stevie." I pull back and stare into her eyes. At one time, she could get me to do whatever she wanted with this same look, but not anymore. "This isn't happening." With my hands on her waist, I easily lift and move her off me. She exhales a whine and pouts her lips. I stand with the blanket wrapped around my waist. "I'm going to take a shower. You're going to get dressed in some real clothes. And don't even think about joining me." Before she can respond, I stomp to my bathroom, the door slamming behind me.

When I get out of the shower, I grab a black Henley and jeans from the stack of clothes I took out of my room last night. My bedroom door is closed, so I assume Stevie has locked herself inside. I yell to her that I'm leaving, but I don't get an answer.

On my way out to my truck, I call Olivia and tell her to meet me at the garage. I owe her a ride on my motorcycle. Today couldn't be any more perfect. The sun is shining bright, and the wind is minimal. Plus, it's the perfect excuse to get out of my house and away from Stevie.

When I pull into the parking lot of the shop, Olivia pulls in right behind me and parks next to my truck. Before she can get out, I'm opening her door and pulling her into my arms. I spin us around before setting her on the ground.

She squeals with laughter. "What's wrong?"

"What do you mean, what's wrong?"

Her piercing blue gaze meets mine. "This isn't like you. I'm not complaining, but it's unexpected."

"I'm happy to see you. And I have a surprise."

Her eyes widen. Not in excitement, but horror. "I'm not big on surprises. One time in college I went to surprise my friend for her birthday, and I was the one that got the surprise. My boyfriend was cheating on me, and I caught them in her dorm room. He told me he went on a guy's trip."

"So, one time?" I raise an eyebrow.

"Not true. Another time I was planning a surprise party for my boyfriend and right before everyone jumped out and said surprise, he dumped me. Right in front of all our friends and family."

I flinch. "That's a little more harsh."

"That's not all. But now can you see why I don't like surprises."

I bend at the knees so I'm eye level. "How about this? I can promise you none of that's going to happen today. Okay?"

Her gaze searches mine, but she reluctantly nods.

"Wait here. I'll be right back." I clasp her cheeks

between my palms and kiss her. Hopefully, that will leave her thinking about me instead of something potentially disastrous happening.

When I told her I'd take her out on my bike, I knew I wanted to take her up to a friend's property along the shore. It's quiet and secluded. The perfect location to spend the afternoon. I rush to my office and grab a small blanket I have tucked away in a closet before returning to the garage. When I reach my bike in the far corner, I load the blanket into one of the saddlebags, then open the smaller of the three overhead garage doors. I hop on my bike and roll it out on to the blacktop.

As soon as Olivia sees my bike, she rushes over to me, the biggest smile lighting up her face.

"Is this my surprise? Are you taking me for a ride?"

"No. We're just going to sit out here and admire it." I give her a teasing smile.

"Smartass." She playfully slaps my forearm.

She looks down at her outfit. "We might have a problem. I think the skinny jeans and t-shirt will be fine, but what about these?" She lifts her foot with the three-inch heel and gives it a shake.

"You'd look pretty hot wearing those while you sit on the back of my bike."

"Is that so?" She gives me a flirty smile.

"Fuck yeah." I wrap an arm around her waist and pull her to me. "Wearing nothing but a white bra and panties and those heels."

"Maybe we can do a photoshoot."

I tug on the collar of her shirt. "What are you wearing now?"

"It's not white but peach."

"No matter the color, I'm sure you'd look hot as hell in it."

I move away and unbuckle one saddlebag and pull out a helmet and boots.

She glances at the items in my hands as her brows furrow.

I shrug. "I peeked at your shoe size and guessed on the helmet. If they don't fit, we can exchange them."

"You bought these for me?"

"If you're going to ride with me, you'll need proper gear. Gotta make sure you're safe." I plop the helmet on her head and buckle the strap under her chin. Bending down, I lift one foot as she uses my shoulder to balance. I remove her shoe and replace it with the six inch black leather motorcycle boot, then I repeat the process with her other foot.

"How do they fit?" I glance up at her, my hand running along her calf.

She wiggles her foot. "Perfect. It's like you're my very own prince charming."

A laugh rumbles from my chest. "Prince and charming aren't exactly words to describe me."

She taps her finger to her chin. "How about badass biker stud?"

"Better."

She holds up her shoes. "Where should I put these?"

"You can put them in the saddlebags on the bike."

Swinging my leg over the seat, I straddle the bike. I turn the key, press the ignition switch, and the engine rumbles to life. I rev the engine a few times before bending over to flip down the foot pads. With a head nod, I motion for her to hop on.

"Um. I've never done this before!" she yells over the chugging of the V-Twin. She stares at me, unsure of what she's supposed to do.

"Put one foot on this pad and hike your other leg over the seat."

"Okay. But wait. Where's your helmet?"

"Don't have one."

She plants her hands on her hips. "That's not going to work. Even badass Jax Teller wears a helmet."

"Well first off, that's fiction. And my primary concern is your safety."

"And I need to make sure you're safe. I'm not getting on until you're wearing a helmet."

"I don't have one, so how about this? If we stop and get one, will you get on?"

"Promise?"

"For you, I promise."

"Okay." A sweet smile covers her face. It's one that makes my heart beat a little faster. She rests a hand on my shoulder and one foot on the pad and lifts herself up. As quick as she can, she swings her other leg over and plops down on the seat.

I turn my head toward her. "Wrap your hands around my waist and hold on. Try not to move around too much because I can feel your movements. Also, when we make turns you want to lean into the turn. Just follow my lead."

"Okay. Got it."

The motorcycle jolts forward, and her grip around my waist tightens. A thrill shoots through me. There's something intimate about having your girl pressed against you on the back of your bike. It's something I can imagine us doing on the weekends. I accelerate out of the parking lot and onto the street, a small grin on my face. She follows all my instructions on not moving and leaning when I lean. Normally, I'm either by myself enjoying the fresh air and clearing my head or I'm with Jay and Archie, but I can see rides with Olivia becoming a regular thing.

We ride our way through the city until we reach the edge of town. Up ahead is an enormous building with a glass front. A giant sign is near the road with a motorcycle sitting in the middle with the Harley Davidson logo on top. We take a sharp right and I pull into an empty parking spot near the front door. I tell her to hop off and I lower the kickstand and do the same. She follows me up to the door as I hold it open for her. Since this place is basically another home away from home, I weave through the aisles right to where we need to be. I pluck a matte black helmet off the shelf, check the size, and tuck it under my arm.

"Ready?"

"Your idea of shopping and my idea of shopping are way different." She laughs.

"No point wasting time. I got what I needed."

"Alright. I'll follow you."

When we get outside and next to the bike, I shove the helmet on my head and she does the same.

"There. Are you happy?" I smirk.

"Very." She runs her fingers along my chest and rises to her tippy toes, placing a quick kiss on my lips. "Let's see what this hog can do!" Her smile shines as bright as the summer sun.

"Just call it a bike." I shake my head but my lips pull to one corner. I straddle the seat, and I direct her to the side as I reverse out. Then I start the engine and motion for her to climb on. Once she's seated, I give it gas and roar down the road.

# CHAPTER TWENTY-ONE

## STRIP ROCK SKIPPING

*Olivia*

As the motorcycle jolts forward, my grip on Ledger tightens. I hug him so tight you wouldn't know where he ends and I begin. We cruise the streets heading North out of town. He takes me on the road that snakes along the shoreline of Lake Superior. I've been on this road many times, but it's different on the back of a bike. The warm sun shining down, breathing in the fresh air, my arms wrapped around Ledger. I can't help the smile that takes over. When I glance in the side mirror, Ledger's lips tip up into a small smile of his own. When we come to a stop sign, he turns and asks if I'm doing alright. I nod, my smile growing bigger.

An hour up the shore, he pulls off onto a narrow paved road and stops at a locked metal swing gate. He plants his feet on the ground, digs into his pocket, and pulls out a key. Turning his head to the side, he asks, "Can you jump off, unlock the gate, and then close it again once I pull through?"

"Yeah."

I climb off the bike and grab the key from him. Once it's unlocked, I push it open. He rolls the bike through, and I secure the gate before hopping back on. The single lane path meanders through the tall pines. Shimmers of light dance on the forest floor through small openings in the trees. We reach a large clearing that sits on a cliff overlooking a small private lake. He comes to a stop and turns off the bike. I climb off and remove my helmet, wanting to get a better view. Ledger is only a few steps behind me.

"What is this place?" My gaze wanders over the crystal blue waters of the lake and the steep cliff that covers one side.

"This is a piece of property a friend owns."

"And he knows you're here?"

He moves to stand beside me. Our arms brush against each other and I look up at him. "He's given me free rein to come up here whenever I want. That's why I have a key. It's a great place to come for some peace and quiet."

I inhale a deep breath of the crisp, refreshing air. You can't get this in the city. "It's beautiful. And you're right. It's so quiet up here."

"It's just us and the sounds of nature." He steps to stand behind me and his arms wrap around my waist. I snuggle into his chest. He uses the opportunity to press a kiss on my neck. Even that slight touch causes my nipples to pebble. I inhale a small gasp when he runs his tongue over the sensitive area right below my ear.

I hum in pleasure before saying, "I bet I could scream your name and no one would hear."

"Only some birds, squirrels, and possibly a moose."

I freeze and then rotate in his arms. "There are moose here?"

"Occasionally. I've seen a few down by the lake before."

My gaze wanders down to the lake. From up here, it looks like a long way down.

"Can we go down there?" I point down to the clear blue water.

"Yeah. There's a trail that zigzags down to a small beachy area. Let's go."

I trail behind him as we head toward his bike. Opening one of the saddlebags, he pulls out a blanket, and tucks it under his arm. He throws an arm around my shoulders, tugging me close. Butterflies erupt in my belly. I love how possessive he gets, even when we're alone. He leads me from the clearing to a narrow path in the woods. Broken twigs and branches crunch under our feet as we follow a worn path until we come across a fallen birch tree blocking our way. Releasing me, he climbs over first, then holds out his hand for me. My fingers wrap around his callous ones as he guides me over the tree.

After a few more twists and turns, we hop over another log, and finally we reach the beach. While it's not the powdery white sand and aquamarine waters I'm familiar with, it's still beautiful. Ledger unfolds the blanket and lays it out on a small patch of grass. He tugs on the corner to make sure it's straight. It's kind of cute that he cares so much about the straightness of the blanket. But when he tugs on the same corner for the fifth time, I stop him with a hand on his shoulder.

"Ledger. It's perfect."

He smooths the blanket one last time before motioning me to sit. I lower myself to the ground and sit cross-legged as he sits down next to me, his long legs stretched out.

I lean over, resting my head on his shoulder. "It's so beautiful here. All we're missing is a picnic."

"Are you hungry? I should have packed something."

I rest my hand on his thigh. "No. This is perfect. Everything is perfect." I rotate to face him. Slowly, I trail a finger on his forearm, tracing one of his tattoos. "Is everything alright? You seem a little … off."

He gives his head a slight shake. "Everything is great. I just want this to be a perfect day."

"I haven't seen this side of you. Are you going soft on me?"

He sits up and grips my chin, forcing me to look at him. His voice is deep and stern. "I promise you, nothing about me is soft."

I've never turned into lady goo as fast as I did with those eight words. Because I know what he's packing and it's not soft. Every day I spend with this man, I fall a little more and a little harder. And I'm terrified. It's been a long time since I've had feelings like this.

With his lips still only an inch away from mine, I whisper, "Not soft. Got it."

When he doesn't move, I'm convinced he's going to kiss me. But he drops his hand and returns to leaning on his palms behind him. Not wanting to show my disappointment, I busy myself with picking at the small rocks that surround us. I pick up a blueish-black rock and brush my thumb over the smooth, flat surface. Rising to my feet, rock in hand, I wind up and side throw it into the lake. As it flies through the air, I hold my breath until it hits the water with a splash. My shoulders deflate. A chuckle sounds behind me and I whirl around. A wide grin covers Ledger's face.

"That's either a sad attempt at skipping a rock or an even sadder attempt at throwing one."

With a hand on my waist, I narrow my eyes. "And you can do better?"

"Pfft. I could do better with my eyes closed and from behind my back."

"Well, Mr. Big Shot. Put your money where your mouth is."

He sits up. A smile tips up on one side of his mouth. "Are you challenging me?"

"Hell yeah." I hold my head up high.

With a slight shake of his head he rises to his feet, a hint of a smile forming on his lips, and stalks toward me. "This is the first time," he eyes me from head to toe, "a five-foot nothing girl has challenged me."

"Five-five." I flash him a cocky smirk.

"Challenge accepted." He bends down and without even looking, he picks up a rock, and stands with his back facing the lake. He grips the flat rock in front of him and flings it as he twists around. The rock skips across the water once, twice, three times before it sinks.

"You did kinda cheat by twisting around but I'll let it slide. Now, show me how you did that!" Bending down, I find another rock, wind up and throw it, but once again it hits the water and immediately sinks.

"Your stance is all wrong." He scoops up a rock and stands behind me. His body is so close, it presses against mine. He grips my hips and rotates me so I'm perpendicular to the lake. "And you need to snap your wrist on release." He flips my hand over and drops the rock into my open palm. His nose brushes against the shell of my ear. Then he whispers, "Feel the rock. Be the rock."

A small laugh escapes me. "Yes, Sensei."

He grabs my wrist and swings it back and forth to the side. "First, we need to loosen you up. Get your body used to the motion."

"There are some motions my body could definitely get used to."

Ledger stops swinging my arm. "Only you could turn rock skipping sexual."

"What can I say? Something with the back-and-forth motion really turns me on." I give him a wink.

He not so discreetly adjusts himself in his jeans. "Back to the task at hand." He pulls my hand to the side. "Now you fling it forward and release right where you want it to land. Give it a try."

Ledger drops back to give me enough room. I repeat his directions over and over in my head. I dig the balls of my feet into the rocks, finding the right position. With the rock smashed between my thumb and pointer finger, I swing my arm across my body, then sling shot it forward, releasing the rock. I hold my breath as it soars through the air and hits the water, skips once, then hits again before sinking.

I scream and jump up and down. "It skipped! I did it! Did you see it?"

"I did." He pulls me to him in a big hug.

"That's the first time I've ever skipped a rock!"

He freezes. "Wait, you've never skipped a rock before?"

"I thought my sinking rocks earlier proved that."

His brows furrow. "You never went to the lake as a kid and skipped rocks?"

"The outdoors and wilderness were never really part of my childhood. Getting dirty, playing in the dirt or skipping rocks wasn't a thing." We had family vacations in oceanside villas. Pools and powdery white sand beaches. Sleeping in a tent with no electricity and especially no flushing toilets didn't exist.

"No offense, but that sounds really boring."

"Oh, thanks." I playfully slap his chest. "But I didn't know anything different. What about you?"

"I basically lived outside. I wandered around every chance I got." He picks up a rock and skips it, and I do the same. This time my rock skips three times.

"Did you see that one?" Delight lights up my face.

"You're a natural."

We continue skipping rocks into the lake. Each one going farther than the last. Pretty soon, it turns into a competition of who can skip their rock the most.

"I have an idea. Any chance of your friend or anyone showing up here?"

Ledger whips a rock, and it skips across the water. "No, I don't think so."

"Let's play a game."

He eyes me skeptically. "What kind of game?"

"Strip Rock Skipping." It was the first thing that came to mind. There's strip poker and strip H-O-R-S-E. Why can't you have strip rock skipping?

He barks out a laugh. "How does that work?"

"We each take turns skipping a rock. Whoever's rock has the most skips, wins and the loser has to remove an article of clothing. Then the first one who's naked has to jump in the lake."

He bends down, his lips inches from mine. "I am going to enjoy watching you jump in the lake … naked."

"Too bad it will be you who's going in naked."

He makes a sweeping motion with his hand. "Ladies first."

Over the next half hour, we take turns skipping rocks into the lake. I'm the first one to remove my shoes and socks, but Ledger is right after me. We continue taking turns, Ledger will go up two and then I'll catch up and he'll have to remove two articles of clothing.

Finally, when we're both down to our underwear, I turn to Ledger. "This is it. Are you ready to get naked?"

"Take your best shot."

I search the ground until I find the perfect rock. I fling it across my body, and it soars through the air, hitting the water and skipping once, twice, three times, and then a fourth before sinking. "Yes! Beat that!" I jump and clap, unable to contain my excitement.

Wordlessly, he picks up a rock, pulls his arm back and sling shots it forward. The rock sails through the air, hitting the water and skips on the surface.

One. Two. Three. Four. And then barely five.

"Oh! Did you see that? I do believe I won that round." He puffs out his chest.

"That last one was barely a hop."

"A hop is a hop. So, what are you losing? The bra? Or the panties? To tell you the truth, I'm not disappointed by either." His fingers dance on the thin strap of my bra.

"I'm sure you're not." I reach behind me and unclasp my bra. The straps slide down my arms. With one hand I take it off and hold it out in front of me and drop it until it falls onto the pile of our other discarded clothes. The warm breeze causes my nipples to pebble. That and being out in the wilderness almost naked with Ledger. His white-hot gaze travels up and down my body, and that also plays a part in the pebbling.

"It's all tied up. This one wins it all." He tosses a rock between his hands. "You can go first."

I pick up a rock and rub the pad of my thumb over the smooth surface. Realizing this is super awkward without a bra, I cross my arm over my chest and sling the rock over the water. It only skips twice before it sinks. Dammit.

He chuckles. "Only two. That's a shame. Guess someone's going swimming."

He picks up a rock and lines up his shot. Sometimes in life you need to play dirty to win, and this is one of those times. I move to stand behind Ledger, so close that my hard nipples graze along his back and I moan.

"Hey!" He turns to look at me over his shoulder. "I know what you're trying to do."

"Do what?" I fake innocence. While he's watching, I run a finger from my collarbone down to the valley of my breasts. Then I circle my stiff peak with the tip of my finger before softly squeezing the tender flesh. "What are you waiting for? Take your shot."

He shakes his head. "Duchess, you're playing with fire."

"And my body is engulfed in your flames."

He gets in position to take his shot. He winds up. Just before he releases, I moan out his name. His rock flies through the air and hits the water once before sinking.

"Oh! I won! Guess who's getting naked now!" I do a little dance before tugging at the elastic waistband of his boxers.

"You cheated. That doesn't count."

"Yes, it does count. It's not my fault you get so easily distracted."

"It's hard to concentrate when you're touching yourself and moaning my name."

"The rules never stated no distractions."

"You just made up the game!" There's a brief pause. A glint of deviousness shines in his eyes. "But you know what? I'm not a sore loser." He hooks his thumbs into the waist band of his black boxer briefs and shoves them to his feet.

He stands on the shoreline in all his naked glory. The silver ball resting on the tip of his cock gleams in the sunlight. And I'm like Pavlov's dog. Instantly, I'm salivating. Including between my legs.

His gaze drifts to mine, eyes narrowing, a wicked smirk stretches across his lips. Then he's prowling toward me.

"Oh no! I don't like that look!" I scream and attempt to run in the opposite direction, but there're sharp rocks, and he's much faster. A second later, I'm hoisted into the air and thrown over his shoulder.

"I decided if I'm going in, you're coming with me. Since you cheated and all." One of his arms clasps around my knees while his other hand smacks my ass.

I squeal with laughter as I attempt to kick and wiggle out of his grip, but it's useless. He's too strong. "This screams sore loser!"

"Well, if you ask me, right now I'm winning. Do you want your panties wet or dry?"

Little does he know they are already wet. But I don't think that's what he meant.

"What?"

"Panties on or off before we go in the water? Nevermind. If I'm going in naked, so are you." He grips the thin fabric and drags them down my legs and tosses them behind him, landing somewhere on the shore near the other piles of clothes.

"Oh my God! You're such a caveman!"

"Admit it. You like when I'm in control." He smacks my bare ass again, but this time he keeps his hand on my skin and squeezes the soft flesh.

I'm hanging upside down over his shoulder as he high

steps into the lake. The water gets closer and closer to my head, the deeper he goes.

His hands grip my hips. "Maybe I should just toss you in?"

"Oh, no you don't!" I wiggle and squirm, trying to free myself, but all I end up doing is sliding down his front. Abandoning my first idea, I go with the next best option. I cling to him like a spider monkey. With my legs wrapped around his waist, and my arms wrapped around his neck, I say, "If I'm going in, so are you."

He thinks for a moment before replying, "I'm okay with that." Suddenly, he hurls his body into the lake. Both of us hit the water with an enormous splash as the lake swallows us up. After a few seconds, we resurface, streams of water running down both of our faces. With one arm still wrapped around him, my other hand swipes down my face.

I giggle. "I can't believe you just did that."

"It was worth it." He brushes away a stray lock of hair from my temple. His steel-gray eyes search mine for a moment before he presses his lips to mine.

# CHAPTER TWENTY-TWO

# TATTOOS & BROKEN HEARTS

*Olivia*

We get out of the water, and he wraps the blanket around us as we sit in a grassy area next to the beach. He wraps an arm around my shoulder while I snuggle into the crook of his arm, basking in his warmth. Slowly, I trace the outline of one of the tattoos on his forearm.

"When did you get your first tattoo?"

He glances up at the sky as he thinks. "I was seventeen. I had a fake ID and wanted to see what I could get away with."

"And it worked?"

He holds out his other arm. "It did. I got this."

He points to a tattoo of a cluster of various sized gears all linked to each other. Ledger continues telling me stories about his tattoos. Some holding more significance than others, like the ones that were dares from friends. When he purposely avoids talking about one in particular, it has me curious.

"What about this one?" I trace the padlock tattoo that covers his chest directly over his heart.

He blows out a humorless laugh. Based on the look on his face, I know it's the one that holds the most significance to him.

"I got this one when I was twenty-five, during one of the lowest points in my life." He bows his head as if thinking about it causing him pain.

Suspicion tells me he got his heart broken, but I want him to be the one to tell me. I reach up, cupping his cheek. The stubble on his face scratches my hand as I turn him to look at me. "I may talk a lot, but I'm a great listener, too."

His mouth tips up in a barely there smile. "Oh, I remember. I had to kiss you to shut you up. Now look where it's gotten me."

"Hey!" I playfully shove his chest, but he grips my wrists, hauling me closer.

"I wouldn't want it any other way." He presses his lips to my knuckles then intertwines our fingers, something he's never done before. His gaze never wavers from our connected hands. "For the first time in my life, I thought I was on the right path. I had my house, my shop, and a girl who I thought I was going to marry." He brushes his thumb over my knuckles. "After seven years together, she didn't want that life, and she left."

"I'm so sorry. You must have been devastated." My heart aches for him. Losing love is never easy. Not that I know from experience, but so I've heard.

"After that, I went out and got the tattoo. Locking up a piece of me since."

"She's an idiot. She didn't know what an amazing man she had. But, if I could, I'd tell her thank you." He tilts his face toward me, eyebrows scrunched together. "Because if she didn't leave, I would have never had my chance with you."

His eyes crinkle in the corners before he exhales a laugh. "Only you could find the good in that."

My gaze meets his. "It's true. What do you say we get out of here? Perhaps, I can show you exactly how excited I am to have my chance with you. Without all the prying eyes from the wildlife. I'm pretty sure I heard a squirrel laughing at me."

"He was just jealous you're mine and not his." He wraps an arm around my shoulder, pulling me into his chest and pressing his lips to my forehead.

We both stand and collect our clothing that's scattered all along the shore. Wordlessly, we get dressed, but I can't help sneaking glances in his direction. How can putting on a shirt be so sexy? It makes me want to rip it off his body again.

We climb up the hill to the bike. Our conversation from earlier flits through my mind. Ledger goes off into the woods to inspect a fallen tree. While he's away, I pull out my heels from the saddlebags and slip them on my feet. When he returns, I'm leaning against his bike, heels on display. We lock gazes and he freezes. A slow smile spreads across his face as he prowls toward me like a hunter stalking their prey.

"What is this?"

"The photoshoot portion of our evening." I grip the hem of my shirt and pull it over my head. Balling up the fabric, I toss it at him. He bends forward to snatch it out of the air and continues strolling toward me until he's right in front of me. I crane my neck up. A smile flirts on his lips.

"You want to do this?"

My teeth sink into my bottom lip. "I do."

"Because we don't have to do it. I don't need pictures when I have the real thing." He raises his hand to cup my cheek. His calloused thumb is rough against my skin.

"It'll be for those nights we can't be together. Now, get out your phone." I playfully shove at his chest and he chuckles but does what I say.

He back pedals, digging in his pocket to pull out his phone. With my legs spread shoulder width apart, I place my palms on the gas tank and peer over my shoulder at the camera. Ledger takes picture after picture as I test out different poses. The way his gaze trails over my body makes me feel sexy and empowered. Normally, I would have never thought to take boudoir style photos, but Ledger brings out my wild side. He makes me feel alive. I'm doing this as much for him as I am for myself. Reaching behind me, I unhook my bra and dangle the strap on my finger. With my other arm, I wrap it around my chest, barely covering myself, and twist half around for a pose.

The first and only time I've been topless outdoors was when we were vacationing in the south of France. Tatum and I were in our early twenties. Being the only ones fully clothed, we felt out of place, so we took off our tops. It lasted a whole ten minutes before our mom approached us, basically called us whores, and told us to put our clothes back on. This time is much different.

"Fuck. I won't need these pictures. This vision of you will be permanently etched into my memory." He reaches down and adjusts himself in his jeans.

A smile spreads across my lips as I continue to pose for the camera. I do some serious ones, others to show my sexy side, and fun and playful ones. This is the most fun I've had in a long time. Ledger is getting into it too, playing photographer. He's directing me how to stand. Where to place my arm. Over a hundred photos later, I get dressed again and exchange my heels for the boots. As the sun draws closer to the horizon, we lock the gate behind us and ride back to Harbor Highlands.

By the time we arrive at the garage, oranges and purples paint the horizon as the brightest stars shine through the darkening sky. He parks his bike outside the garage door and we both hop off. I collect my things from the saddlebags and replace them with my helmet. I won't need that unless I'm with Ledger. He moves his bike inside and closes and locks the garage when he's finished. I prop myself against the door of his truck, not ready for the night to be over.

He strolls over to me and wraps his arms around my shoulders, pulling me to him. "I enjoyed spending the day with you."

"Your company wasn't so bad," I tease.

"Oh, is that so?" He drops his arms to under my butt and lifts me. Using his truck for leverage, he nestles his hips between my legs as I wrap them around his waist.

"So, what now?" Before he can respond, an inhuman sound rumbles from my stomach. Heat creeps up my neck as I silently pray the noise wasn't as loud as I thought it was.

"It sounds like I better feed the angry beast that lives inside you." He chuckles. I drop my forehead to his shoulder, mortification taking over. "It's okay to have a gremlin living inside you. Doesn't make you any less beautiful."

I jokingly slap at his chest. "You're such a jerk. Just for

that, I get to pick what we have. Should we get takeout and eat it at your place?"

He lowers me to the ground. "Takeout sounds great. But how about we go to your place instead?"

# CHAPTER TWENTY-THREE

## JACK & ROSE MOMENT

*Ledger*

My heart stopped when she said she wanted to go to my place. Thankfully, she agreed to go to hers instead. Stevie needs to leave, and quick. I hate having to lie to Olivia. And it's best if they don't know any more about each other than they already do. While I picked up the takeout food, I used that alone time to call Archie to see where the hell he is. When he didn't answer the first time, I tried again. Luckily, he answered the second time. When I asked him where he was he said he got delayed with car troubles but he should be back in a couple of days. All I saw was red. I told him to hurry his ass up then hung up. I didn't want to deal with this shit to being with and now it's for a few more days. I'm about ready to send a search party for him. After

I left the restaurant, I took the long way around to Olivia's to give myself a few extra minutes to cool off.

Bags overflowing with Chinese food containers fill both my hands as I let myself into Olivia's house, stroll past the living room, and into the kitchen. Placing the food down on the white granite countertop island, my gaze wanders around the open kitchen. Olivia's nowhere in sight. I unload all the containers from the bags and set them on the counter when she comes strutting down the stairs, her hair pulled up into a ponytail, wearing a worn shirt and short cotton shorts.

"Oh my god. That smells delicious." She wraps her arms around my waist.

I glance down at her, recognizing the faded black shirt she's wearing. "Did you steal my shirt?" I love seeing her wear my clothes. Hell, she can have my entire wardrobe as long as I get to admire her in every threadbare t-shirt and color faded hoodie.

She looks down, then meets my gaze. "Yes." She lifts the collar up to her nose and inhales. "I like that it smells like you."

I shake my head. "I don't know what I'm going to do with you." Actually, I know exactly what I want to do with her, but food first.

"You can figure that out later. I'm starving." She pulls out plates and silverware while I get us a couple glasses of water. We sit at the island, passing containers of food between us until our plates are overflowing.

Olivia props her elbow on the table while stabbing a piece of broccoli. "What made you want to become a mechanic?" She pops the sauce-covered vegetable into her mouth and chews.

"As a teenager, it kept me out of trouble. The more I did it, I found I enjoyed the challenge of taking engines apart and putting them back together. And it turns out I was good at it." I shrug and take a bite of my kung pao chicken." What about you? Do you like working as a receptionist?"

"It's … alright." She slumps in her seat. "It was a lot more fun when I worked next to Charlie. Parisa's still there, but she's so busy I rarely get to see her besides a passing wave." She pokes at a piece of chicken with her chopsticks. "I'll be honest, it wasn't something I aspired to, but my dad forced me to do something. At the time, it worked out."

"What do you want to do?" I glance at her while I chew.

"You know … I'm not really sure. I've never really thought about it."

I raise a questioning eyebrow.

"I know. I know." She throws her arms in the air. "What thirty-one-year-old doesn't know what she wants to do with her life?" She pauses. "This is going to come off as spoiled rich girl, so hold your judgement."

I hold my hands up in defense.

"I never had to really think about it. My parents always made sure I had enough money in my bank account. They paid for my house and my car. They wanted me to get a job, so I found the first place that hired me. It appeased them enough, so I just carried on as normal."

"Okay. Well, that still doesn't answer my question. What do you want to do?"

She sits up straighter in her chair. "One thing I've always enjoyed is helping my mom plan and host all her charity functions. I don't exactly enjoy working side by side with my mom because she can be a bit much, but I enjoy working with the caterers and the decorators."

"So, party planning?"

There's a brief twinkle in her eyes. "Yeah. I guess so.

Event coordinator has a nice ring to it. I enjoy creating and organizing these magical nights that no one will forget."

I set my fork down. "Why don't you do that, then?"

"An event coordinator?" She glances up at the ceiling. Her lips purse as she tosses the idea back and forth in her head. "Maybe. But I don't know where to start."

"You're resourceful. I bet you could figure it out. You already know all the people and have the connections. You just need to put yourself out there."

Her gaze drops to her plate as she pushes chicken and broccoli around.

"How about this? I'll be your first client."

Her head flies up, eyes meeting mine. "You want to throw a party?"

"Sure. It'll be an easy one, too. Only two people on the guest list. Location: your bedroom. And all you have to worry about is dessert."

A tinge of pink covers her cheeks as she smiles. "Oh yeah. And what's that?"

"You. In fact, I want that right now." My fork drops to my plate with a clatter. In one swoop, I'm lifting her from her stool and carrying her into the living room.

"Hey, I wasn't done with that." She giggles.

"You are now."

I toss her on to the couch and climb between her spread legs. My fingers dance at the waistband of her cotton shorts. "I'm craving something sweet. Think I'll find it here?" I kiss the fabric covering her pussy.

She nibbles on her bottom lip. "I don't know, but you should find out."

The next morning, I stir awake with Olivia's limbs wrapped around me. A mound of blonde hair drapes across the pillow and over my arm that she's currently using as a pillow. Fuck. Having her body pressed up against mine in heaven. I don't remember sleeping next to a woman feeling like this. After I carried Olivia to the couch, we ended the night with me giving her two orgasms, and then she got on her knees to give me one of my own. Then both of us passed out.

She stirs awake, stretching her body, causing her to press her chest into mine. Her eyes flutter open and bright blue eyes greet me.

"Morning." My voice is deep from sleep.

"Good morning. I'm happy you stayed."

"There's nowhere else I would rather be." And that's not a lie. The more time I spend with her, the more she consumes me. I never expected her to completely wreck me the way she has. Every waking minute, I want to be by her side, holding her. Kissing her. Smelling her sweet jasmine scent. I want all of it.

"Last night was amazing."

I run my fingers up and down her bare back. "It was."

"But we forgot something."

"What did we forget?"

She rises to her knees and hikes one leg over my hips so she's straddling me. "Last night we got dirty, so now it's time we get clean." She glances down and winks, but then she's moving across me, taking the sheet with her. Once she's standing, she peers over her shoulder at me like the tempting seductress she is. "Are you joining me?" She releases her grip on the sheet and the silky fabric floats to the floor, pooling at her feet.

In a daze, all I can do is stare as she saunters into her en suite bathroom … naked. Then it hits me what she just said. When a woman asks you to shower with her, you do it.

I scurry out of bed and race into the expansive bathroom. On one wall is an enormous Jacuzzi tub, a marble top double sink vanity sits in the middle. Then she's standing in front of an open glass door with the water spraying out of a flexible shower head hooked on the wall. The inside is all tile with a glass wall facing us. A stone bench sits along the back wall and a rain shower head hangs above.

"This is one hell of a shower, especially for one person."

"It's my orgy shower."

My eyes go wide. She said it so nonchalantly, I'm unsure if she's kidding or not.

A laugh bubbles out of her. "I'm joking. But right now, I want two of us in here." She pushes a button and the shower head above rains down. She steps inside and tilts her head, causing the water to cascade down her body, trickling down the valley between her tits. She brings her hands up to smooth her hair back.

I can't help the groan that escapes. "Duchess, you really know how to bring a man to his knees."

"Come in here and show me."

Not waiting another second, I drop my boxer briefs to my feet and join her in the shower. Once inside, I step directly in front of her. I wrap my hand around the nape of her neck and haul her to me, slamming my lips down on hers. She yelps in surprise but it quickly turns into a moan as I deepen the kiss. The water pours down, cocooning us from everything. She wraps her arms around me, holding me close. My grip tightens when she rubs herself against my now hard dick. She kisses me with fervor. A throaty groan escapes me when her hand travels between us and wraps around my cock. She gives it a gentle squeeze before pumping me once. Twice.

She breaks away from our kiss. "Have I ever told you how much I love your piercing?"

Before I can say anything, the pad of her thumb brushes over the head with the ball at the tip. I inhale a sharp breath. On her next swipe over the head, a groan rumbles in my throat.

"Have I told you how much I like when you stroke me?"

"By the look on your face, I can tell exactly how much you like it."

I slam my mouth to hers. With my hands on her waist, I walk her backward until her knees hit the edge of the bench. I direct her to sit down. I don't break our kiss until she's seated.

I squat down in front of her and hike one of her legs over my shoulder. Her legs spread open for me, her pretty pussy on display. My hand glides up her smooth thigh until I reach her pussy. "Mine," I growl before thrusting a finger into her opening. Her moans echo off the tile and mix with the splashing water. I pull out and push back in. Her hips buck against my hand. "You like that?"

"Oh God. Don't stop." Her voice is low and husky. Her fingers wrap around the edge of the marble bench.

"I have no intention on stopping until I bury my cock deep inside filling you up." Her pussy clenches around my finger, telling me she wants that, too. I pull out and add a second finger. Except this time I bend down, wrap my lips around her clit and suck.

She screams out my name while grinding against my mouth. Her fingers are now white knuckling the bench.

"Ah! Oh! Don't stop. I'm going to come." She continues to buck against me harder and faster. I insert a third finger, stretching her even more. I alternate between lapping at her wetness and sucking on her clit. The way her legs tremble, I know she's close. She rocks her hips against my face. Her grip on my shoulder length hair tightens as she guides me to the exact spot she wants me. Then her orgasm rips through her, my name echoing off the tile walls. I continue to lap at her pussy, wanting every drop of her. Once her moans and gasps subside, I slow my pace and eventually stop. When I glance up, her chest still heaves from her climax.

"I don't know why, but every orgasm gets more and more intense with you."

"Just so you know, I'm not done with you yet." I haul her to her feet and spin her around. "Palms flat on the bench." She does what I say. The creamy flesh of her ass sticks up in the air. With my palm, I can't help but redden her delicate skin. As soon as my hand makes contact, she yelps, but I bring my hand down and swirl a finger through her wetness. Suddenly her yelps turn into moans. I repeat the process on the other side because they need to match. The loud smack sound bounces off the tile, followed by another moan when I plunge a finger inside her.

"Do you think you're ready to take my cock?"

"Yes. Yes. Fuck. I want your cock."

"What do you say?"

"Stick your cock in me before I do it myself."

I can't help the laugh that escapes. "You always take what you want. I like that. I won't keep my good girl waiting."

I grip my dick and run the head up and down her slit. The metal ball at the top runs along her clit and she moans. I repeat the motion, except this time she pushes her ass back against me, needing more. On the third time, I find her entrance and thrust in. She whimpers from the intrusion, but soon enough, she's moaning. I pull out and drive into her, loving the way her tight pussy grips me. I ease out before slamming into her, causing her palms slide forward on the bench. After she regains her position, she pushes back, meeting me thrust for thrust. One hand grips her waist as I rest the other against the glass wall for balance. I continue plunging in and out of her. My grunts mix with her moans. This girl consumes me in every way possible. My hand slides down the glass and grips the other side of her hips. I pull out of her, and she whimpers from the loss. Lifting her to a standing position, I turn her around. For so long, I've denied myself this intimacy. I never wanted it. Until now.

"I want to see your face as you come on my dick." Rotating us, I take a seat and guide her between my legs. My hard cock juts out between us. The silver ball on the tip glistens in the dim light. She nibbles on her bottom lip before hiking one leg over my knee, resting it on the bench. Then she does the same with the other. I reach between us and grip my shaft as she lowers herself down inch by glorious inch.

"Oh! Shit!" she gasps as she continues down until she's fully seated.

I inhale a sharp breath.

"I'm so full. You're so deep like this. And your piercing …"

I buck my hips up, and she arches her neck and moans. Slowly, she rocks her hips, her moans and whimpers tell me she's loving it. She brings her hands up to my shoulders for better leverage.

"Duchess, you better get moving because with the way your pussy's strangling my cock, I'm not going to last long." I grip her waist and guide her to move, but she doesn't need my assistance. She picks up the pace, sliding up and down my hard cock. The sounds of our pleasure mix together in the enclosed shower. Two become one. Mind, body, and sounds. With an arm wrapped around her, I bring my other hand up to cup her breast. Then I'm bending down and sucking a hardened nipple into my mouth. My tongue swirls around the stiff peak before I gently bite down.

"Oh fuck. That feels so good," she mumbles between pants.

I repeat the process on the other nipple and this time, her pussy contracts around me. Her speed picks up as she uses my dick to pleasure herself and I'm enjoying every second of it.

"Ah. Yes. Right there. I'm so close." Her pants become more shallow before her pussy contracts around me as her orgasm takes over.

"Keep riding me, duchess. I'm right behind you." I move my hands to her hips, my fingertips digging into the soft flesh as I guide her down on my dick.

She continues her pace, riding my cock. "Ledger." Her eyes squeeze shut. "I'm going to come again."

My balls constrict as a tingle creeps up my lower back. I grunt, thrusting up, exploding inside her as another orgasm ruptures through her. She slows her pace until she finally stops with me still inside of her.

She gets up to move, but my grip on her waist tightens. "Fuck. I just want to feel you like this for a few more seconds."

Her gaze meets mine. "Okay." Her hands thread through my hair at my temples, finger combing the wet locks.

It's been so long since I've felt this. This connection. But it's deeper than sex. And fuck if I ever want it to stop.

"Is that your handprint smeared down the glass?"

I turn to the right to look at what she's talking about. "Yeah. I guess so."

She chuckles. "That's very *Titanic* of you."

I raise an eyebrow in question.

"Jack and Rose? In the car? Got all steamy? Never mind." She grips the side of my face and presses her lips to mine in a chaste kiss. "We better get to the actual showering before I run out of hot water."

We take turns lathering each other up and rinsing off. I never imagined something so simple would be so intimate. It's been years since I've had feelings that have come remotely close to what I feel for Olivia and that shit scares me the most.

# CHAPTER TWENTY-FOUR

# NOT JAY'S GIRLFRIEND

*Olivia*

The past week has been one of the best I've ever had. Since the weekend of the motorcycle ride, we've been inseparable, minus when work got in the way. Every night we'd end up in my bed, on my couch, on the kitchen counter, and once on an Adirondack chair in my backyard. Which is one hundred percent not meant for two people ... having sex. Now, it's Friday. I took the day off work—or called in sick—cough, cough. By now I would consider it bad luck if we didn't see each other. It's like a reading streak on your e-reader. You'll go to extreme lengths so you don't break it. My plan for today is to surprise him and see if he can spare a couple of hours.

I park my SUV in an empty spot in front of his shop. At first glance, I notice his truck isn't parked out front, but that's not uncommon. He could have parked inside the garage. With my purse tucked under my arm, I hop out and make my way to the steel door. When I yank it open, the fluorescent lights buzz above me, but the shop is eerily quiet. Usually, music is blaring through the stereo or the clanking of metal echoes around the massive area. But today, nothing. A truck that's not Ledger's sits in the far bay while a car is parked next to it. I cautiously meander through the garage, hoping to run into someone. "Hello?" I call out.

A shadow catches my attention, then someone steps out from behind a truck. I spin around, expecting to see Ledger, but it's not the tall, broad frame I'm familiar with. Instead, she's my height, maybe a little taller, raven colored hair that drapes down one shoulder and down her chest. A full sleeve of tattoos covers her left arm visible from the black, low-cut tank top she's wearing. My gaze continues to wander down to her dark purple shorts, fishnet stockings, and black boots that are absolutely adorable.

"Oh. Hi." My gaze drifts up, still unsure how I should perceive her. I fidget with my bag. "Are you getting your car fixed?"

"No," she deadpans.

*Maybe she's Jay's girlfriend? Does Jay have a girlfriend?*

"I'm here for Ledger." She rests a hand on her hip.

*Not what I wanted to hear.*

"Oh." My eyebrows shoot to my hairline. "You're here for Ledger?"

"Yeah. We're longtime friends." She tilts her head and narrows her eyes, studying me.

"I see," I mumble, more to myself.

For my entire life, I've caught people in situations where they shouldn't be. An intern in my dad's office after hours. My mom's best friend's son sneaking out a window

175

when she's the only one home. It's something I'm all too familiar with and it's unsettling. This reminds me of one of those times.

"How do you know Ledger?"

How do I answer this? We never really had the talk. "We're friends."

"Based on the look on your face right now, I'd say you're more than just friends." Her hand falls to her side.

"Uh. Um. Something like that. By the way, is he here?" My heart hammers in my chest as I glance around. Something's not right. When my gaze returns to the woman in front of me, she tilts her head to the side as if she's trying to figure out who I am. Like I'm the one who needs a reason to be here and not the other way around.

"He stepped out but should be back shortly."

I nod slightly. "When he comes back, tell him I stopped by." I turn and walk away, but quickly backtrack. "Olivia. I'm Olivia."

"I'll tell him you stopped by Olivia." She flashes me a smile somewhere between sweet and snarky, and it causes bile to creep up my throat.

I whirl around and smack into a hard chest. Woody, rich sandalwood with a hint a grease assaults my nose. One whiff, and I know exactly who it is.

Ledger pulls off his aviator sunglasses and hooks them into the collar of his black t-shirt.

"Son of a bitch," we whisper at the same time, but mine's laced with a little more venom.

# CHAPTER TWENTY-FIVE

## UNCOMPLICATE IT

*Ledger*

It was risky leaving Stevie alone in my garage. Even riskier that I never mentioned her to Olivia. Of course, they just so happen to meet when I leave for ten fucking minutes. When you play with fire you don't just get burned, you go up in flames.

"Oh good. You brought breakfast. I'm famished." Stevie saunters toward me.

Everything plays out in slow motion. Olivia turns toward Stevie and watches her every move, then her gaze sling shots to me. A storm cloud of grays and blacks brew behind her normally bright blue eyes.

I shove the bag toward Stevie. "Take it and go eat in the break room."

Quickly, she clutches the bag to her chest before it falls

to the floor. "You're not joining me?" Her voice is sweet as she bats her eyelashes. She knows exactly what she's doing and if it were anyone else, I would put her in her place, but I can't with her.

"Just go," I grit through my teeth.

"You know, I kinda want to stay here. See how this plays out." She opens the bag and digs inside.

"Just fucking go!" I clench my fists.

"Alright. Alright. I'm going. Don't get your panties in a bunch." She crumples the top of paper bag closed and drops it to her side. "It's great to meet you, Olivia. Hope to see you around." With that, Stevie sashays across the garage and down the hallway toward my office.

"What the hell was that?" Olivia screeches. "Please don't tell me you're sleeping with her too? Oh my God." She doubles over, clutching her stomach. "I think I'm going to be sick."

I inch toward her, unsure what I should do. "No. I'm not sleeping with her."

She rises to her full height, glaring daggers at me. In an instant, she's stalking toward me and shoves at my chest. She may be small but she still manages to push me off my balance.

"I know we never said what this …" she points between us, "is, but at the very least, I was expecting it to be exclusive. Then I show up and you have another girl here! What the hell!?" She shoves me again.

This time, I clasp her wrists in my hands. "It's nothing! I'm not sleeping with her."

"Then who the hell is she and what is she doing here?" She rips her hands from my grasp.

I blow out a breath. "She's … It's … complicated."

"Well, you have five seconds to uncomplicate it for me." She stands tall with her arms crossed over her chest.

"She's the daughter of a good friend. She went missing for a few weeks and then showed up at the shop, needing a place to crash."

"And where is she staying?"

"I thought about here—"

"You're making her stay in a dirty, dingy garage?"

"No. She's staying at my house."

"She's staying with you!? What the hell, Ledger!" She paces in front of me.

"You have nothing to worry about."

"You only have this gorgeous, bad ass Barbie staying with you, but I have nothing to worry about." She throws her arms in the air.

"Hey." I grip her chin and bend down to her eye level, forcing her to look at me. "I only have eyes for you."

Her face softens for a moment, but the moment doesn't last long. She pulls out of my grip. "No. You don't get to sweet talk your way out of this." I can see the wheels turning behind her irises as she thinks about everything that happened the last few days. "Wait. Is she why you canceled on me a week ago?" When I don't answer her right away, she continues. "I can't believe it! You lied to me. You've been lying to me. For over a week!" She paces in front of me, then stops, her face flush. "That's why you always want to go to my house instead of yours."

Once again, Stevie comes into my life and fucks it up. "I was hoping she'd be here for a day, two max and then everything could go back to normal. You two wouldn't even know about each other."

"So you wanted to keep it a secret? What else haven't you told me?"

Fuck. Do I just tell her and get it over with? She's already mad. How much worse can it get?

"She's also an ex-girlfriend." Her jaw hits the floor.

"Before you say anything, it was a long time ago. She is nothing to me besides a buddy's daughter. That's it."

Her mouth opens and closes a few times. "And I'm just supposed to believe you?"

"Have I given you a reason not to?"

Her eyes widen as I've said the most asinine thing. "Based on everything that's happened in the last ten minutes, I'd say yes."

"Alright. I deserve that." I huff out a deep breath and lean against the back door of the car. "About a month ago, a friend came into the shop. He told me he hadn't heard from his daughter in a week. This is typical of her, so he didn't think too much of it. Anyway, he gave me a heads up in case she showed, which has happened in the past, but it's been years." Olivia stares at me, but the tension in her shoulders drops a little, so I continue. "Then, out of the blue, she showed up here. My friend was out of town looking for her, so she needed a place to stay."

"She couldn't have gotten a hotel room? There are plenty around here."

"As bad as it sounds, I needed to know where she was until Archie can get her."

Her arm brushes mine as she moves to stand next to me. "And she's an ex?"

"She is."

"And nothing is happening?"

"Nothing."

She nibbles on her bottom lip as she contemplates her next words. "Wait. Is she ... is that tattoo because of her?"

All I can do is nod.

"Okay. It would have been better if you told me instead of blindsiding me. How would you feel if my ex showed up, and I didn't tell you?"

My nostrils flare just at the thought of another guy near her. "I'd kill him."

"So you get it."

"Look …" I turn and grip her waist and move her so she's standing in front of me. Bending my knees, I get down so I'm at eye level with her, which isn't too far considering the heels she's wearing. "I'm sorry. As bad as it sounds, I didn't want you two to meet. She's my past. I want you to be my future."

"This is … a lot. I need some time. Time to think. Process all this." She wraps her hands around herself, head bowed. Moisture collects in the corners of her eyes. She tries to blink away the tears, but they don't go unnoticed.

I push off the car and move to stand in front of her wanting to hold her in my arms but she sidesteps me. With her head still head bowed, she slides past me. No goodbye. No we'll talk later. And not a single glance back.

Stevie steps out from the shadows. "That didn't sound like it went well. Hungry?" She holds the paper bag with a sandwich inside out to me.

I glare at her. I'm one thread away from snapping. Every time she enters my life again, shit gets all fucked up. This time, she's ruined the best thing that's happened to me.

# CHAPTER TWENTY-SIX

## TAKE OUT THE TRASH

*Olivia*

After the run-in with Ledger's ex, I needed time to myself. On my way home, I stopped at the store and stocked up on all the carbs and sugar imaginable. Empty calories for my empty heart. My two-day solitude comes to a halt when there's a knock on my door. When I don't answer, Tatum lets herself in with her key. Charlie trails close behind her.

Tatum scrunches her nose. "What's that smell?"

I glance around my living room. A couple of empty take-out containers and dirty dishes collect on the floor next to the couch and end table. "I don't smell anything."

"Oh God. You're used to it." Tatum storms past me and Charlie shrugs as she follows along. Tatum throws open a window to let in some fresh air while I curl up on the couch and cover myself, including my head, with a blanket.

"What are you doing?" Tatum rips the blanket off me.

"Hey! I'm wallowing."

"It's been two days of you ignoring us and living in this filth. This isn't like you." Tatum glares down at me with a hand on her hip.

Charlie exits the room and a few minutes later returns with a garbage bag and collects all the trash. "This is your one pass. In fact, you get five more minutes, then you're taking a shower and telling us what's going on."

True to her word, Charlie gives me exactly five minutes before she's gripping my wrists and tugging me off the couch.

"I'm up. I'm up," I whine. "When did you get so strong? Is Bennett having you bench pressing two by fours?" She narrows her eyes and pushes me out of the living room. Sluggishly, I climb the stairs until I reach the bathroom attached to my bedroom. Stripping out of my clothes, I turn on the water. Before it warms up, I step into the spray. It's only then I let everything go. Tears run down my cheeks, blending in with the water pouring down on me. I've kept every guy at arm's length. Every single one. Except Ledger. He's been the only one who's sparked joy in my life. Marie Kondo type of joy. There is something about him I need. Desire. Crave.

Once all my tears dry up, I squirt some coconut shampoo into my hand and run it through my hair. The suds run down my legs and wash away into the drain. When I finish, I step out and dry off. I find a pair of yoga pants and like it's second nature, one of Ledger's old shirts I borrowed … or stole. After tugging it on, I finger comb my hair before throwing it up into a messy bun on the top of my head. When I descend the stairs, my living room no longer looks like a garbage can threw up. A vanilla cupcake scented candle is lit on the coffee table masking the previous stench.

Tatum pats the couch cushion next to her. "Now that you look a little more human, sit. Tell us what happened."

I take a seat between Tatum and Charlie. "Thanks for cleaning." I glance between my two friends.

"Something had to be done. Now, what happened?" Charlie rests a hand on my arm.

"Where do I start?" I blow out a long breath. "I met Ledger's ex."

"That's … awkward," Tatum says.

"Just a little, but that's not all. She's been staying at his house."

"What the hell!?" Charlie screeches.

"That's the first thing I thought, but with a few more expletives. Needless to say, I've been suffering from emotional whiplash. I need some time to think everything through." Even though during my time alone, I didn't do much thinking. I ate junk food and binge watched *Friends*. Also, Ross and Rachel were on a break. Oh shit. Does Ledger think we're on a break? I told him I needed time alone. That totally constitutes as a break. I scramble off the couch and dash into the kitchen.

"Where are you going?" Tatum asks as she and Charlie jump up and follow me.

I swipe my keys off the counter. "What if Ledger thinks we're on a break? Nothing good comes from a break."

"You're going to see him? Looking like that?" Tatum asks.

I glance down at my outfit that's more fitting as pajamas than going out in public, but I don't care. I can't spare another second. "Yes." I yank open the door and dash to my SUV. If I know Ledger, he's at his shop. With the gas pedal to the floor, I race across town. Possibly breaking a few speed limits and maybe rolling through a stop sign or two, but I need to get to Ledger.

I hop the curb in my SUV as I speed into the parking lot. My tires screech as I step on the brake, my bumper inches away from hitting the side of the building. I slam the shifter in park and beeline it to the door. Charging through the doorway, I quickly glance around. The lights are on, but no one is in sight. "Ledger!" I peek under a car. "Ledger!" I peer around the hood of a truck. Nothing. Then a noise catches my attention. But it's not coming from the shop area. I freeze to get a better listen. It's hard to hear over the hammering of my heart. Hushed moans sound from the hallway. I tiptoe toward the noise.

"Oh! Yes! Harder!" Followed by grunts come from behind a closed door. Ledger's office door.

My entire body goes numb. I can't believe he's doing this. At the first opportunity, he sleeps with his ex-girlfriend. If I didn't tell him I needed space, would this have happened? No! This isn't my fault. I'm not the one fucking someone else. My fists clench.

My face heats red hot as I bolt down the hallway and across the garage. I shove open the door and before I can make it outside, I run face first into a solid chest. Sandalwood and grease swirls around me.

"Olivia?"

My hands ball into tight fists and deliver the first blow. "You piece of shit! How dare you!" I continue hammering my fists into his chest. "I can't believe I trusted you!"

"Hey. Hey! What are you talking about?" Ledger tries to control my wrists, but I continue swinging my hands.

"You're sleeping with your ex!"

"No. I'm not."

"Yes! You are! I heard you! In your office!" I continue to flail my arms.

Giving up on trying to control my wrists, he wraps me in a bear hug. "Olivia. What are you talking about? I'm not sleeping with Stevie."

My chest heaves, as much as it can while being squeezed by Ledger. Then it hits me. He's right here. He's not in his office. "I thought I heard you having sex in your office."

"Right now?"

I nod. He releases his grip and stomps across the garage. I chase after him. Once he's at the door, he raises his fist and pounds on the wood. "Get the fuck out here right now!"

Murmurs and rustling sounds from the other side. Ledger continues beating on the door until it finally opens. Jay exits first, straightening his shirt. A smug smile on his face as Ledger glares at him. Next, Stevie stumbles out, her hair tousled, fastening the button of her skirt. Before she can get past Ledger, he grips her wrist, stopping her.

"I want you out," he seethes.

"Fine. I'll just go back to your place."

"No! I want you out! Out of my garage. Out of my house. Out of my life."

"Where am I supposed to go?"

"I don't give a shit. Since you're fucking Jay now, you can stay with him because I'm done."

"My dad won't be too happy that you threw his daughter out on the street," she counters.

"I'll deal with Archie. In fact, I'll call him right now." He pats his pockets, looking for his phone, but comes up empty.

"Don't worry about it. I'll call him." Stevie slides past Ledger. She glowers at me as she passes.

Both Ledger and I spin around and watch as she leaves out the door. When she vanishes, Ledger blows out a breath and scrubs his hand down his face. He storms down the hallway toward the garage. His gaze is on me, but I can't read his expression. It's a mix of hurt and betrayal. The only issue is I don't know how much of that is because of me.

# CHAPTER TWENTY-SEVEN

## IF YOU LOVE SOMETHING...

*Olivia*

I help Ledger search for his phone around the shop, his truck, office, and we even drive to his house, but come up empty handed. While he runs to the store to get a new one, I get a bucket of bleach water and clean his office. Jay comes in and helps me scrub all the surfaces.

"You should bleach your dick, too, while you're at it." Ledger's large frame fills the doorway.

"Hey man. Sorry. It didn't mean anything." Jay stands to his full height.

"I'm not worried about that. But my office?" The corner of Ledger's lips tip into a smile as he shoves Jay's shoulder.

"It wasn't my idea. I was just a willing participant." Jay laughs.

"Isn't that always the case?" After Ledger is done staring Jay down, his gaze meets mine, indifference etched on his face.

"I'll take that as my cue to leave. I have a car to finish up." Jay tosses his rag into the bucket and strolls out of the office.

Once we're alone, I turn to Ledger. "Did you get a new phone?"

"I did."

Unsure how he feels about me attacking him earlier, I decide to face it head on. I rest my hand on his forearm. "I'm sorry. I made a snap judgement. This is all so hard to navigate." I pause. "Also, just so we're clear, we weren't on a break."

"A break?" His eyebrows squish together.

"You know what? Nevermind." I wrap my arms around his waist and press my cheek to his chest. "Can we just go back to how everything was before I ran into Stevie?"

His hands trail up and down my spine. "Yeah. I like that idea."

The next day as I'm leaving work, my phone buzzes with a message from my mom. She wants me to pick up and drop off some documents regarding the decor rental for a charity dinner. After I pick up the folder, I make my way to my parents. When I reach their driveway gate, I stop and punch in the code. The wrought iron gate rolls to the side and I drive up the driveway lined with maple trees. The three-story brick house comes into view. I park my SUV on the circular driveway at the front of the house. I grab the paperwork from the passenger seat and hop out. Strolling up to the arched doorway, the smell of freshly cut grass fills my nostrils. On the outside, the house resembles a life people would be envious of, but on the inside, it's anything but.

Stepping into the expansive open foyer, I'm met with the smooth, white marble floors blending in with the pristine white walls. Growing up in this house, I was never aware of the starkness that surrounded me, until now. It resembles more of a museum than a home. Folder in hand, I make my way down the hallway, past the formal living room that's never used, and into the open kitchen. My mom's sitting at the island, her blonde hair wrapped in a bun so tight on the top of her head the Botox doesn't need to work to keep her face wrinkle free. Phone in hand, she's scrolling away. I'm sure it's to find her next vacation destination that won't include my father. The man who funds the trips, but never goes, sits at the dining room table, reading glasses perched on his nose as he reads *The New York Times*. *The Wall Street Journal* lays on the table next in line.

"I have the papers you wanted." I hold up the manilla envelope before setting it on the counter in front of my mom.

She glances from her screen to the folder in front of her before meeting my gaze. "Thank you, dear. It's always such a hassle to get back into town."

"No problem. I was in the area anyway."

"Have a seat." She pats the stool next to her. As I pull out the stool and sit, she sets her phone down on the counter. "How have you been?" Before I can answer she switches topics. "I had lunch with Mary, John Callahan's wife, the surgeon. Well, their son just moved to the area to open a pediatric office. I think you two should go to the Wine on the Water event together. It would look very good if you showed up on his arm for this event, especially since you ran out early during the last one."

All the socialites in the community attempt to outdo one another with their extravagant charity events. Wine on the Water is my mom's biggest event of the season. She rents out a giant yacht that parades around the harbor. Mostly it's just another excuse for people to get drunk and write it off. For charity, of course.

"It's not my fault there was bad shellfish." The lie rolls off my tongue. Something I've learned from my mom. "Plus, there's someone else I want to ask."

Her eyes light up. "Oh yeah, who's that?"

"My boyfriend, Ledger."

"Boyfriend?" My mom tilts her head to the side. "You never mentioned a boyfriend."

"It's new and we're seeing where it goes." It's hard to fight the smile that fills my face when I think of him.

"What the hell kind of name is Ledger?" my father asks behind his newspaper from the table behind us.

Ignoring him, I keep my attention on my mom. "He's kind. Compassionate. He makes me laugh and smile. Plus, he owns his own successful business."

"What kind of business?" my father asks.

I glance toward him and square my shoulders. "He runs his own mechanic shop."

"Certainly doesn't take an ivy league education to do that," he murmurs under his breath.

I spin around on my stool. "You know what? It doesn't. But he's successful. And he did it all on his own and no one can take that away from him."

He methodically folds the newspaper and sets it down on the table next to him. His gaze bores into mine. "I did not bust my ass to provide a life for you, only to have you slumming it with some mechanic. You are better than that.

Look at your sister. She's dating one of the top lawyers in the state. He's the kind of man you should be with. Not some mechanic."

The venom in his tone sends ice through my veins. It's never mattered to me what Ledger does or doesn't do for a living. I'm drawn to the connection we have, not what's in his bank account.

"Your mother has arranged a date with the Jonas Callahan. I expect to see you there with him," he says.

"But he's not my boyfriend. Ledger is my boyfriend, and he's the one I want as my guest." I stand my ground.

He stands and moves to the island in front of me, palms pressing on the granite countertop. "This is a big event for your mother. It's best you don't go embarrassing her or me. The campaign will be picking up soon. Everyone will be on their best behavior."

I roll my eyes. How dare I live the life I want, instead of the facade of the perfect senator's daughter he expects? "That's right. This is, after all, about you. Maybe it's best I go by myself. Even better, maybe I don't go at all. God forbid, I don't fit into the perfect mold you've constructed for me." Hurt and rage bubbles up inside me. It's like a dormant volcano. Years and years of buildup and now it finally explodes. All I see is red. I shove away from the counter, the stool clattering to the ground. Not bothering to pick it up, I march down the hallway with heavy footsteps, slamming the front door shut with a loud bang.

Before I can reach my car, an arm on my shoulder twists me around. I yank out of my father's grasp and step backward.

"I've had enough of your attitude. Have some respect." he seethes. When I say nothing, he continues, "Now, you'll do as I say. And that includes stop seeing the mechanic."

"And what are you going to do if I don't?" I spit out.

He gets in my face, his words a venomous whisper. "I'd hate for him to lose that shop he's worked so hard to build."

My heart stops. He wouldn't, would he? My gaze flits back and forth, searching his for any telltale sign he's bluffing, but his expression is like a stone statue. Exactly like his heart. I'd expect a lot of things from him, but to take away someone's livelihood?

"Now your mother has arranged a date for you. So, you'll be there on Jonas' arm. And break up with the boyfriend. We can't have the gossip mill whispering about how you're a whore. Got it?"

I ball my fists together, my nails digging into my palms so hard I'm surprised I haven't drawn blood. I can't believe he has the audacity to speak to me like this. We glare at each other. Hatred burning in both our irises. I itch to fight him, to call his bluff, but then I'd be gambling with Ledger's livelihood, and I can't do that. Because I know his threats are not empty ones.

He pulls away. "Finally, for once you listen to me. After everything I've given you." Then he marches toward the front door. After it slams shut behind him, I turn on my heel and storm away.

Once I'm in my car, I'm out of the driveway as fast as the car can move. This is the first time my parents have spoken to me like that. Granted, this may be the first time I've ever defied them. I've lived my entire life under their thumb. I know the things they are capable of. Mostly my father. I don't know if I'm ready to find out the repercussions.

When the adrenaline wears off, tears flood my eyes. With the road a blur, I pull off on the shoulder and let everything out. My life is a complete mess, and I don't know what to do anymore. The one thing that makes me happy drives a wedge into everything else. My parents will never approve of someone like Ledger. They look down their noses at people like him. I wish they could see how happy he makes me, but clearly happiness means nothing to them.

After the tears subside, I flip down the mirror and check my makeup. Mascara streaks down my cheeks. So much for being waterproof. Digging in my center console, I find a packet of tissues and clean it up. Then I riffle through my bag to find my compact and reapply a fresh coat of makeup. At least now it's only the red puffy eyes that give away that I've been crying. When I'm situated again, I realize I'm only a few blocks from Trey's house and right now I could really use a friend.

Five minutes later, I'm pulling into his driveway and parking next to his Escalade. I jump out and take the sidewalk up to the front door. Before I can raise my hand to knock, the wood door flings open. Trey looks casual, wearing dark jeans, a Porter's T-shirt, and his signature sexy smile.

"To what do I owe this pleasure?"

My eyebrows pinch together. "Um. What's on your head?"

He reaches up the plastic cap making a crinkling sounds as he taps it. "Shit. I forgot about that. It's my twice a month honey and olive oil treatment."

"So that's why your hair is so soft. Why didn't I think of that."

"I'll give you my recipe. So, what bring you here?"

My shoulders slump and I exhale a deep breath. "Why couldn't things have worked out between us?"

Wordlessly, he steps out of the way, giving me enough room to walk past him. After I enter, he closes the door and follows me into his living room. I take a seat on one side of his brown leather sectional, and he sits two cushions away from me. A moment passes before he says, "Um. I don't know if you want me to answer your question or if it was rhetorical."

I flop against the back of the couch and throw my arm over my eyes. "I just left my parents. We got into a huge fight about how I'm a big disappointment."

"How is that possible?" The couch cushion next to me dips as Trey moves closer.

"Ledger." I sigh. "And how we're dating."

"Ah. So, if you were dating someone like me, that wouldn't be an issue."

With saying a word, I tap the tip of my nose. "The Wine on the Water event is this weekend. As much as I don't want to be there, I need to be, but there is no way I can bring Ledger as my date."

"I can always be your date." He wiggles his eyebrows.

My forehead creases. "Did you forget how well that turned out last time?"

He laughs. "Fair enough. I have my own ticket anyway, so it doesn't matter. You've never been one to back down from a challenge."

"As much as I would love to piss off my parents right now, I just can't. Plus, they want me to go with some surgeon's son." I drop my head to my hands. "Maybe I need to cool it with Ledger. At least until things settle down." Plus, it might jeopardize his business, but I don't tell Trey that.

"Is that what you want?"

"It's not about what I want, but what's best for the situation. You don't understand what my dad is capable of. Hell, I'm terrified of what he might be capable of." I clasp and unclasp my hands in my lap.

"So, you're not going to mention the event to Ledger? If I recall, that didn't go over very well either."

"It's a lose-lose situation." A giant pit sits at the bottom of my stomach. When did life become so complicated? I need to make a decision and time is running out. Ledger loses his business, or I lose Ledger. And there's only one obvious choice. My heartbeat thunders in my throat. I can't believe what I'm about to say. I peer up to Trey. "It's hard to take you seriously with that on your head." Trey shrugs. "But I know what I have to do."

# CHAPTER TWENTY-EIGHT

## IT'S ALL DIFFERENT

*Ledger*

Using a rubber mallet, I tap on the front axle bolt. With my concentration on the motorcycle, I don't hear anyone come into the shop until a dark shadow casts over me. Glancing up, I shield my eyes from the sun, and Olivia's small frame comes into focus. Her tan legs on display leading up to a pair of denim shorts and a tank top that hugs her chest. It takes everything in me not to lift her up on my tool bench and bury my face between her legs. The scowl on her face tells me she didn't come here for a ravishing.

"Hey duchess. I wasn't expecting you today." I rise to my feet and find a rag to wipe my grease covered hands.

"I need to talk to you," she says, apprehension in her voice.

My eyebrows pinch together, and I lean against my tool bench, crossing one foot over the other. There's a shift in the air. Something is wrong. I know it. "Well, talk."

Her gaze drops and locks onto the cement floor. "I can't do this anymore. Things are too complicated and you're right," finally her eyes meet mine but hers are void of any emotion, "we are from two different worlds. This would never work out between us."

I can't help but laugh. "You're joking, right?"

"I'm sorry. I just can't—"

I stand up straighter. "You're lying."

"Ledger, I'm sorry." She's looking in my direction, but it's more like she's looking through me and not at me. The conviction in her voice is lacking, as if she rehearsed the words.

In two steps I'm chest to chest with her. I grip her chin, forcing her to meet my gaze. "I know you. I know you're lying."

"Please don't do this."

"I'm not doing anything." I drop my hand to my side. This time, moisture collects in the corner of her eyes. But I know it's not because she's leaving. It's because of whatever reason she's convinced herself that she needs to leave, even though, I know she doesn't want to.

She looks down at her tangled hands. "I'm sorry." Then she spares me a glance before she twists around and runs out the overhead door. I hear the roar of the engine start up, then she peels out of the parking lot.

What the hell just happened?

For the rest of the week, every time I call Olivia, it goes straight to voicemail. I go to her house and either her car isn't there or she doesn't answer her door. I was half tempted to kick it down, but I also don't need her neighbors calling the cops on me. Plus, she has security cameras so if she's inside she knows it's me, she just doesn't want to answer. When I stopped by her work, I was told she was out sick, which again I know is total bullshit. The last thing I need is to make a scene.

Instead, I went home. Now I'm sitting on my couch with my phone in hand, willing it to ring or buzz with a text message from her. Something else happened. There is no way she would just up and leave, especially saying so few words. But what else can I do? Jack rubs his head against my ankles, then turns around and does the same on the other leg. He jumps up on the couch and meows at me, his one eye boring into mine.

"I know buddy, I miss her too." I run my hand over the top of his head. He pushes into me and purrs. Jack walks across my lap to the other side of the couch, looks up at me, and meows again before he does a circle and lays down where Olivia would normally sit. "You're good company, but it's not the same." He rests his chin on my leg and I continue to pet him. It was never supposed to be like this. This is why I don't get close to anyone. It fucks with you and throws your entire life into a tailspin. I've had too many of those in my life and I don't need anymore. But with her it's different. It feels different. She's different.

# THE GOLDEN TICKET

*Ledger*

It's Saturday afternoon. I'm sitting on the couch with a beer in one hand, the remote in the other, and staring at a blank tv screen. I never thought this would be my life. That I would be the guy pining for a girl ... again.

A knock on my front door pulls me from my sad and depressing thoughts. I contemplate if I should answer it or not. Truth be told, I'm not in the mood for any company, but then again, what if it's Olivia. The knock sounds again, and I jump to my feet. My heavy footfalls thud on the floor as I rush to the front door. Twisting the knob, I throw it open. All excitement dies when Trey stares back at me.

"What are you doing here?" I frown.

"Saving your ass. Now can I come in?" I narrow my eyes at him, then my gaze drifts down to a bag draped over his forearm. When I don't answer him, he continues. "It's about Olivia."

I step to the side, and he strolls in past me. He does a three-sixty, taking in my kitchen. It doesn't have any state of the art appliance or high end counter tops but everything is functioning and serves a purpose.

"Wow. I've never been in your house." He nods his head as he glances from one side of the room to the other, taking everything in. "This is nice."

"If you came over here to tell me that, you can get the fuck out." I cross my arms over my chest.

"Actually, I didn't. But I did come here with purpose. I know we've never been close, but Olivia means a lot to me and despite what she said, you mean a lot to her so …" He digs in his back pocket and pulls out a white envelope with gold foil trim, holding it out to me.

"What's this?" I glance down at the paper.

"An invitation to my birthday party."

My head shoots up as my eyebrows knit together.

He laughs and wiggles the envelope at me. "Just open it."

I flip the envelope over and pull out the flap holding it closed. A light blue piece of paper with gold trim catches the light. Slowly, I pull the paper from the envelope, still unsure of what it could be. Wine on the Water fills the top of the page in a script font.

Again, my eyebrows crease. "This is the event Olivia's mom is hosting."

"It is. And Olivia is going to be there."

At that, my ears perk up.

He taps the paper. "That's your ticket in."

"Wait. Aren't these events like black tie or some shit? Because you won't find any of that in my closet."

"I got it covered." He holds up the bag draped over his arm.

"We're sharing clothes now?"

"You can be grateful for my help, or you can stay home and sulk while some other guy gets your girl."

My girl. It has a nice ring to it. No matter how hard I try, I know Olivia is not the type of person you just forget. She burrows herself into your soul and sets up camp. At least, that's what she's done to me.

"She needs someone to go after her. To fight for her. She needs you."

His words sink in, but there must be an ulterior motive. We never do favors for each other. Not growing up and definitely not now. "Why are you doing this? We've never helped each other."

"I love her like …" He pauses and glances up to the ceiling, deep in thought, before continuing. "I would say like a sister, but we kissed and that would be weird. She's one of my best friends. She deserves all the happiness, and as odd as it is, you make her happy."

The corner of my mouth tips up. "So, you're saying I win?"

He snorts. "I'm letting you win. Now, take this before I change my mind." With his arm stretched out, he holds the garment bag to me. "Also, you're on your own for shoes. While we're about the same build, the shoe size is a different story."

I grab the bag and walk to my bedroom. Once inside, I kick the door shut behind me. Carefully, I pull the fabric from the bag. I inspect the black suit. I run my fingers down the lapel. That's when I spot the label above the inner pocket. Giorgio Armani. While I'll admit I don't know much about fashion, I do know that this suit cost more than my entire wardrobe. I strip out of my clothes and step into the slacks. I fasten the waistband and throw on the white dress shirt. Starting at the bottom, I button each iridescent pearl button, leaving the top one undone.

I pull open the door to my closet and pull out a pair of black boots. Since I own nothing with a fancy label, these are clean and will have to do. Shutting the door to my closet, I take a seat on the bed and shove a foot into each boot. I tie up the laces and straighten the hem of the pants, covering the top of the boots. When I stand, I find a small mirror that's tucked into the corner. I run my fingers through the long strands of hair at the top, smoothing it out as much as possible before pulling it back and securing it with a hair tie. The hair and the boots are the only thing that gives it away that I don't belong. And maybe the tattoos on the top of my hands. Also, the one crawling up my neck. Maybe it will be too dark for anyone to notice.

Once I'm finished, I head out to the living room, my boots thumping across the wood floor to the same rhythm as my heartbeat.

"Who knew you could clean up?" Trey glance up from his phone.

"Fuck off." There's a brief pause. "Also, thanks for this. The suit and the ticket. Also, for telling me about Olivia."

"No problem."

"I really appreciate it." I hold out my hand for him to shake.

He glances down before gripping my hand with his. Then he does something that catches me off guard. He pulls me to him and wraps his other arm around me, slapping my shoulder.

"Just treat her right."

We pull away from each other. "Believe me, once I get to her, I'm never letting her go."

He glances down at his watch. "Shit. You better get going. The boat's going to be leaving the dock soon."

Quickly, I grab the suit jacket and throw it over my shoulder. Trey exits and I lock the house up behind him. Before he gets in his SUV, he stops. "Also, I'll send you the dry cleaning bill when I get my suit back."

I shake my head. He gets in his vehicle and reverses out of my driveway. Once I'm in my garage, I manually raise the garage door. I toss Olivia's helmet into one of the saddlebags and shove mine on my head, buckling the strap under my chin. I push my bike out, fire it up, and then close the garage door. With traffic and parking, I figure it will be easier to maneuver around on the motorcycle. I throw a leg over the seat and rev the engine a few times before lifting the kickstand and taking off down the road.

Desperation races through my veins as I take the bike on a wild ride through the city, weaving between cars and trucks honking their horns. I can't miss the boat. Finally, when I reach the marina, I spot the massive yacht still at the dock. Calling it a boat is an understatement. I twist the throttle grip and speed into the parking lot. I know my time is running out. I race up and down the rows of cars, praying for an empty spot. When I rounded the corner of the last row, I spot a sliver of an opening, just enough for a motorcycle between the curb and another car. Without hesitation, I take it. I kill the engine and toss my helmet on the passenger seat, not caring if someone steals it. My focus is to not miss the boat. My feet pound on the blacktop as I run across the parking lot. I notice the dock crew tearing down the velvet ropes and I run faster.

"Wait! Wait!" I flail an arm as my boots continue to

slap against the ground. When I reach a podium, I double over, hands on my knees to catch my breath.

"Are you here for the event?"

My chest heaves as I reach into the inside pocket and pull out the invitation Trey gave me and wordlessly, I hand it over.

The attendant checks the ticket and then peers over the podium to me, still doubled over. "You made it just in time. But I wouldn't wait too much longer."

I rise to my full height. My breathing is still a little shallow. "Thanks."

They direct me to a ramp. An attendant follows close behind me as I climb up. Once I'm on the boat deck, the gate locks with a clank. As I glance around, groups of people mill about, mingling with champagne glasses and low balls in their hands. Most of the women eye me with curiosity while the men glare with skepticism. Moisture collects on my palms, and I do my best to wipe them discreetly on my slacks. But at this point, there's a good chance I'll rub a hole through the fabric before my palms are dry.

The boat jerks forward, and I reach for the railing. I suck in a sharp breath through my mouth and slowly blow it out of my nose. Quickly, I scan all the unfamiliar faces on the deck and my blonde duchess is nowhere to be seen. I peer down as the boat cuts through the inky water. That was a bad idea.

I pinch my eyes shut as a wave of nausea washes over me. I need to get off the deck. She's not out here, so she must be inside. I unclench the railing and trail behind a middle-aged couple across the deck as they enter a set of double doors that open to a grand staircase that leads down into the ballroom. I scan the room, pausing briefly at each table to see if I can spot her. But table after table I come up empty. The loud chatter of conversation from the fully packed ballroom does nothing to mask the thumping in my chest. It's going to take me all night to find her. But then I see her. My heart stops and everything else disappears.

# THE GOLDEN TICKET

## Ledger

I twirl the base of my wine glass on the table, watching the red liquid swirl around before lifting it to my lips and taking a drink. This is my second glass of wine and I'm about ready for the third, but who's counting? I should feel proud of the event. It's been a tremendous success. Hundreds of thousands of dollars have been raised for charity. All the guests raved about the food. But the most talked about has been the grand ballroom with its lavish decorations and shimmering lights. The dark cherry wood offers a beautiful elegance while the white table and chair linens, make it appear bright and airy. An enormous chandelier hangs from the center of the room, the light reflecting off its crystals and illuminating the grand staircase at the bottom of the steps. Yet here I am, alone, all the while my thoughts are consumed by only one man.

"Why do you look like you want to be somewhere else right now?" Tatum takes the seat next to mine and replaces my empty wine glass with a fresh one.

"Thanks." I hold up my wine glass before taking a giant gulp. "Would it be bad if I said I wish I was?"

"Not at all because same."

I glance around the room before turning my attention back to Tatum. "Where's Adam?"

Her gaze drifts down to her wineglass for a moment. "Oh, he couldn't make it. Something came up with work." She takes a long drink of her wine.

Something tells me it's not work related, but I don't press it. This has been two events now where he hasn't showed. I know Tatum will tell me what's happening, but on her own terms. If it's not soon, I'll resort to prying the information from her.

"Olivia, there you are." My mom prances up to the table, the Rene Ruiz slate blue off the shoulder gown shimmers in the low lighting, a younger man on her arm.

As I stand, I roll my eyes, making sure only Tatum can see. The last thing I want right now is my mom trying to play matchmaker again. When I face them, I flash my mom a tight-lipped smile.

"I want you to meet Jonas Callahan." She brushes her hand down his bicep like she's petting a cat. By the look on her face, she's the one purring. "Jonas recently opened up his own pediatrics office in town. Isn't that right?" My mom gazes up adoringly at Jonas. If she was twenty years younger, she'd probably try to date Jonas. Who am I kidding? She'd date him right now. Married or not.

I hold out my hand for Jonas. His grip is firm, but his

skin is much softer than the familiar calloused ones I'm used to. A pang of sadness flows through me. For the first time in my life, I finally figured out what I want, but I can't have it. What kind of kick in the crotch is that?

"Nice to meet you, Olivia." His voice is smooth like an aged scotch. Too bad my tastes have changed, and I would much rather have the bite from a tequila shot. No training wheels. He's attractive with sandy blond hair and piercing green eyes, but he's not the guy for me.

"Likewise, Jonas." His grip on my hand never wavers, maybe for a beat longer than normal. In most cases, I would take that as an invitation for more to come, but Jonas isn't the one I want more from.

"Sorry I wasn't able to pick you up beforehand. Things got crazy at the office right before I was scheduled to leave. A young mother came in with her infant who had a terrible cough. I couldn't leave until I could reassure her everything would be fine." His features soften.

"That's quite alright. The infant is certainly more important in this situation."

"Maybe I can make it up to you. I can take you out to dinner sometime."

"Oh. Um—"

"She would love that," my mom answers for me.

My muscles tighten and my jaw clenches as I glare daggers at her, but she doesn't notice me since she's too busy doting on Jonas. She asks him questions about his practice and while Jonas rambles on, and I can't help but be bored. It's like his voice could lull anyone to sleep. My gaze wanders off to find something more interesting, but then my heart stops and I forget how to breathe. At the top of the grand staircase, peering over the railing, is Ledger. Even from a distance, his steely gray eyes bore into mine.

Without a second glance back, I excuse myself as they continue talking. My pace quickens with each footfall as Ledger descends the stairs. My smile goes wider with each passing second. All I want is to be wrapped in his arms. That's all I want. For a man who doesn't smile, like ever, he's also wearing one of the biggest I've seen. My heart hammers in my chest as we draw near. It's only a few feet, yet it seems like miles. Finally, he's so close I can smell his signature sandalwood scent with a hint of grease. Without hesitating, I throw myself into his chest, wrapping my arms around his neck. He pulls me tight to him, arms wrapped around my waist. I gaze up into his eyes, and it feels like home. Not wanting to wait another second, I kiss him. I kiss him as if I'm never going to kiss him again. Slowly, we pull away. Still love drunk from his lips on mine, I somehow manage to ask, "Why are you here?"

Not missing a beat, he says, "There was a time when you showed up at my house and declared you weren't going to let me go. I'm here now, doing the same thing."

My heart jumps to my throat. I've never had a guy do something like this for me. To chase after me like this because he wants to, not because he has to. "You're my knight in shiny combat boots."

He presses his lips to mine. "Here to sweep you away from the evil castle."

"You can't sweep me away if I go willingly."

"That would make it easier than me throwing you over my shoulder and carrying you out of here."

"I can always pretend." There's a brief pause. "But seriously, how did you get in? Tickets are five-hundred dollars apiece and have been sold out for months."

"Let's say someone with more expensive tastes than me came over to my house with a ticket and a suit."

I pull back and gaze down at his chest. "I didn't notice

the suit. Armani looks good on you. This looks like something Trey would wear. Did he?"

He nods. "Don't get used to it. But also, would now be a bad time to say I'm terrified of boats?"

He sets me down on my feet. "Wait? You're afraid of boats?"

His body tenses. "When I was a kid, there was an incident with a pontoon boat with too many people on a windy day. The boat capsized, sending everyone into the water. Since then, I've avoided boats."

I softly cup his cheeks, brushing my thumb over the light stubble wanting to divert his attention back to me. "And you still willingly came onto a boat to be with me?"

The lines on his face soften as his gaze searches mine. "I wasn't going to lose you."

I pull him toward me and kiss him. I don't care who sees. What others will say. I've only known this man for a short time, but already he's done so much more for me than all my previous boyfriends combined. I want everyone to know he's mine.

Someone behind us clears their throat. I pull away from Ledger and look over my shoulder. My father is glowering, and my mom is standing next to him. I'm not sure if she's checking Ledger out or judging him.

"This isn't the time or place for that type of behavior." My father scolds me like a teenager who got caught making out with her boyfriend. Technically, half of that is true.

I reach down and intertwine my fingers with Ledger's. "This is my boyfriend, Ledger."

Ledger reaches his hand out. The cuff of his suit jacket rides up, exposing his tattoos. My father glances down and his lip snarls. If he was trying to hide his disappointment, he didn't do a very good job. Reluctantly, he lifts his hand and gives Ledger's a shake. When they break apart, my father discreetly brushes his palm on his suit jacket. I can't help but roll my eyes at his behavior. This is something I'd expect from children, not a grown adult. But I guess they've always made it apparent they don't like outsiders and Ledger is as outside of their circle as it gets. Then my mom holds out her hand. Ledger takes it and brings it up to his lips and places a soft kiss on the top of her hand. The quietest squeal escapes her throat, followed by a blush I've never seen. My father pulls her away and she frowns.

"Olivia. I would like to speak to you." He glances at Ledger. "In private."

My grip on Ledger's hand tightens. "Whatever you have to say to me, you say in front of Ledger."

Ledger bends down and whispers in my ear. "Duchess, it's okay. I'll be right here."

"Are you sure?"

He nods and untangles our fingers. A part of me doesn't want to go without him because I'm slightly terrified of what my father has to say. With Ledger by my side, I know I would have someone in my corner. Someone who would stand up and fight for me, fight with me, if I needed it.

I reach up on my tippy toes and kiss his cheek and whisper, "If I'm not back in ten minutes, come looking for me."

The corner of his lips tips up in the shyest of smiles. "I will always look for you."

My father motions his head for me to follow him. I trail in his footsteps, but glance over my shoulder to Ledger, still in shock that he's actually here. I turn around and continue following him. We weave in and out of the crowd until he finds a secluded spot at the bow of the ship. He spins around. "What the hell is happening? Didn't we tell you not to bring him? He doesn't belong here."

"Trey gave him his ticket and told him to come here for me. And what's the big deal? He's not doing anything wrong."

"Did you not see the people staring?" He sweeps his hand in the direction of the ballroom. Then his face is inches from mine. "He's drawing unnecessary attention."

"If people are staring, that's their problem. And the only unnecessary attention that was drawn to us was when you came over saying we needed to talk," I snap back.

He flinches, unsure how to handle my response since I never talk back to him, but he quickly recovers. "I won't stand for this disrespectful behavior. Did you already forget what I told you? Lose the boyfriend."

I glance around, eyes wide. "We're on a boat. Where are we supposed to go?"

"Figure it out. Why can't you find someone like your sister?" he mutters under his breath.

I scoff. "Where is her boyfriend right now? I haven't seen him. You talk so highly of him, but have you met him? I know I haven't. At least Ledger made it a priority to come."

"He's a very upstanding gentleman who's very busy with his job," my mom says.

All I can do is roll my eyes. It's ridiculous she believes that. If either of my parents would open their eyes, they would see they're not happy. Their children are not happy. At least I wasn't until now.

My father steps up to me. "This isn't about Tatum's boyfriend. This is about yours. He's not the type of guy you should be with. Did you know his mom is in jail for selling drugs? Did you know he's also spent time in jail? Do you know how that looks on me? On this family?"

"I know all about Ledger's past. And it's the past for a reason. We all have one. We just happen to have enough money to make certain things in our past disappear. Like the time Mom drove drunk and crashed into a telephone pole. You went out to pick her up and said you were driving and swerved to miss a deer. Or how about that time when you—"

"That's enough!" he snarls. "I've worked hard to give this family everything and you just want to throw it away for some punk who isn't going anywhere in life."

"His name is Ledger. He runs his own successful business and he works hard for everything he has. We could all learn something from him." Including myself. I don't say that out loud, but the more I think about it, those words have never been more true. Maybe it's time for me to step out of my comfort zone. Ledger is the person I aspire to be. Strong. Independent.

My dad gets in my face, eye level with me. "This is the last time I want to see him at a charity event. Next time, I'll throw him out myself." Before I can say anything, he storms past me. My mom is close on his heels. My blood boils. How long have I had these blinders up to not realize this is my life? I don't want to be like them. I never want to be like them. Turning on my heel, I stomp out to the ballroom. Instantly, I spot Ledger, exactly where I left him, and a little part of me sighs in relief. The closer I get, I can't fight the smile that takes over.

When I reach him, I take his hand in mine. "Let's get out of here."

"We're on a boat. Where exactly are we going?"

"We'll go find a closet so I can make you forget we're on a boat." I tug on his hand.

"Shit. I won't argue with that."

"I didn't think so."

He trails behind me as I meander through the crowd, hand in hand, not caring about the hushed voices or glaring stares. I would take this man on one of these tables just to prove he's mine, but I won't. Toward the bow of the yacht, I remember seeing a closed door that might be a closet. I guess we'll find out.

## CHAPTER THIRTY-ONE

# THE BEST DISTRACTION

*Ledger*

Olivia leads me down a dark corridor before stopping at a closed door. She rests her hand on the doorknob and glances up at me. Twisting the metal, with her gaze still locked on mine, a smile flirts on her lips. She pulls it open and tugs me inside. Blindly, both of us reach around, searching for a light. My finger grazes a switch and I flick it up. An overhead light flickers to life, illuminating the cramped area. Shelves filled with linens, toiletries, and other miscellaneous items cover all three sides of the closet.

Her fingers grip the lapels of my jacket and pull me toward her. "Have I told you how hot you look in this suit?"

"Better enjoy it now because I won't have it for long."

"I fully intend to." She tugs me down, slamming her lips to mine.

I cup her cheeks, holding her to me. All thoughts of being on a boat dissipate. My focus is solely on this amazing, strong, feisty, beautiful woman in front of me. One who has stuck around for me. Now I want to show her I'm here for her.

Her hands brush up and down my chest and over my shoulders. My hands drop to my sides so she can remove the suit jacket. The fabric hits the floor with a thud. Slowly, I drag my fingers up the back of her dress until I reach a small, metal zipper. Before I can tug it down, she pulls away.

"This is about you." Her bright blue eyes meet mine.

"Whatever you have planned, it would be better if you do it naked." I grip the zipper again and slowly drag it down. When she doesn't fight me, I finish pulling it all the way down. One strap at a time, I brush the fabric off her shoulders until it floats to the floor, pooling at her feet. My breath hitches as I take in the sight before me. She's in a white, lacy, strapless bra and matching lace panties. I fight the urge to rip everything off her and worship her body. My dick twitches in my pants. She steps toward me and out of the dress. I kick it away. With a featherlight touch, I run my fingers up the side of her rib cage. Goosebumps prickle her skin in my wake. When I reach her bra, I cup her tits. They're heavy with desire in my palms. My thumbs graze over her nipples until they're stiff peaks under the lace. In one swift movement, I pull the fabric down under each breast causing them to push up. She gasps in surprise as the cool air washes over her heated body and I want to hear all her noises. I love how her body responds to my touch. Bending down, I suck one pebbled nipple into my mouth, swirling my tongue around while my fingers pinch the other one. Her moans and whimpers grow louder when I bite down.

"Ledger. Oh my God." Her words come out in breathy pants.

"You're so responsive to my touch. I bet I could make you come without touching your pretty pussy." I pinch her nipple again.

"Yes." She arches her back, thrusting her chest into me farther.

I reach around her, my fingers at the clasp holding her bra together, and she pulls away.

"I want you in my mouth."

"My good girl wants to choke on my dick?"

A devious smile covers her lips and my cock twitches from that single look.

"But I want to see your tattoos while I do it." Starting at the top, she pops the button of my dress shirt. She works her way down, one by one, until she's brushing the fabric over my shoulders and until it drops to the floor. She crouches, dragging her fingers down my chest, but stops halfway down. Her warm lips press against my chest, right over the padlock tattoo over my heart. My muscles tense. The gesture is simple, but fuck, it does things to me. She continues her descent until she's eye level with my bulge. Her fingers trace the outline of my thick dick as it strains against the black slacks. Not wanting to wait any longer, she pops the button and tears down the zipper. She peels the sides away and lowers the waistband to just below my ass. Her hand rubs me on the outside of my boxer briefs. With each stroke I grow harder, which I didn't think was possible. I hiss a sharp breath through my teeth when her thumb brushes over the metal ball on the tip.

"Fuck, duchess. You got me hard as steel. Pull me out. I want to see what I look like sitting on your tongue."

She does exactly as I say. Her thumbs run along the elastic waistband, then she gazes up at me through her lashes. With her eyes locked on mine, she tugs the band down. Once the fabric passes my bulge, my dick bobs in front of her. Her tongue peeks out, wetting her lips. She's practically salivating to suck me off. She's hungry for me, and who am I to deny her any longer?

I run one hand through her hair and grip the back of her head. "Open your mouth and stick out your tongue." She obeys my orders. I glance down and she looks so beautiful in front of me, mouth opened wide, waiting for me. I'll give her every piece of me and more. She looks up, eyes meeting mine. With my other hand, I grip my dick and run the head along her tongue before thrusting in. She whimpers when I pull out.

"My good girl wants my cock." Her blue eyes sparkle with lust as she nods her head. I run the tip of my dick along her plump, red lips. "Tell me how much you want it."

"I need your cock so bad."

"What do good girls say?"

"Please," she begs.

"That's right. You make me so hard when you beg." I guide the tip to her parted lips, and she wraps them around the head, sucking me in. I drop my head and groan. My hand falls away, and she takes over, guiding me in and out of her mouth. Her tongue swirls around the steel ball, mimicking the motion of my tongue on her nipple earlier. "Fuck duchess. If you keep that up, I'm going to explode."

She hums around my dick and the vibration shoots right to my balls. I thread my hand in her hair and hold her as I tunnel in and out of her mouth. Her moans spur me on. I continue thrusting in and out, hitting the back of

GIA STEVENS

her throat each time. "Swallow my cock. Show me how much you want it."

Her hands wrap around to the back of my thighs, her nails digging into my flesh as I continue thrusting in and out of her mouth. My movements slow and Olivia takes over. She brings her hands up front and wraps one around the base of my dick and the other massages my balls. The double sensation sends a tingle down my spine. Her hand moves in time up and down my shaft with her lips. At the tip she swirls her tongue and then pushes down, twisting her hand.

"Fuck. That's it. I'm not going to last much longer." My words spur her on to move faster, and that's my undoing. Heat spreads through my body and I jerk forward as my orgasm detonates. White hot heat flashes behind my eyes. Olivia sucks me down as my hot cum spurts out, hitting the back of her throat.

My movements slow as my orgasm subsides. She continues sucking my cock, making sure not to miss a drop. When she's done, she kisses the tip of my still semi-hard dick. Then she wipes at the corners of her mouth as she rises to her feet.

Before she can get too far, I wrap an arm around her waist and tug her to me. "That was … fuck." But what I really want to tell her is that she's amazing and I'm falling in love with her. Instead, I press my lips to hers, then whisper, "Now it's my turn to repay the orgasm."

Her breath hitches when I trail my hand down her stomach and dip inside her panties. The pad of my finger connects with her clit, and she sucks in a breath and exhales a moan. I swirl my finger around the tight bud. "You're soaked for me. Does sucking my fat cock make you wet?" She spreads her legs, hiking her knee to my hip, opening herself up to me.

FLIRTING WITH THE BAD BOY

"Yes." She moans when I plunge a finger inside her opening. I thrust a few more times before inserting a second finger. She grinds her pussy against the palm of my hand, taking what she wants.

"Ride my hand. Show me how much you want it." Her pants and whimpers grow louder as her orgasm builds. I continue thrusting my fingers in and out, her arousal coating my hand. I love how wet she gets for me. Her hand rests on my shoulder for support. Her nails dig into my skin. I'm sure I'll have half-moon indentations in my flesh by the time we're done. I bend down and suck one of her nipples into my mouth and bite down, and she explodes on my hand.

"Oh Ledger. Right there. Yes." Her hand flies to the side searching for a solid surface to keep her steady, but instead she hits stacks of individually wrapped toilet paper that tumble to the floor.

"Duchess, you need to be quiet otherwise everyone is going to hear how much I make you moan," I whisper.

She sinks her teeth into my shoulder in an attempt to stifle her screams. I continue my thrusting as her pussy grips my fingers. Her whimpers subside and I slow my pace. I pull my hand out and my fingers glisten with her arousal.

"Open up." I hold my fingers up to her mouth and her lips part. I run my fingers over her tongue. "Suck." She wraps her lips around my fingers and licks off her arousal. I pull my hand away and slam my lips to hers, wanting to get a taste of her from her own lips.

I pull away, my lips centimeters away from hers. "Fuck, duchess. Your taste is my new favorite drug. Now to feed my addiction." I bend down, but she stops me with a hand on my shoulder.

She glances down at me, eyes hooded. "You're

insatiable. But there's no way I'll be able to stay quiet again. Plus, if we're gone any longer, I'm sure someone will find us."

Rising to my feet, I nuzzle my nose along her neck. "Fine. But once we're back on solid ground. You're mine. I want your voice hoarse from screaming my name."

"I'm holding you to that."

# CHAPTER THIRTY-TWO

# JUST SAY NO

*Ledger*

As soon as the boat returned to the dock, I was the first one off. I put Olivia on the back of my bike, and we rode out of there and straight to my house. Before I could close the front door, she pounced on me. Over the next twenty-four hours we barely left my bed. Of course, we traded multiple orgasms, but also, I enjoyed just laying with her in my arms. Every second I spend with her, the more she imbeds herself in my soul. I thought I could keep her at an arm's distance, but now I'm finding that to be impossible. She was hesitant to tell me about her dad's threats toward me and my shop. But I reassured her I'm not scared of him or any of his threats. I'll go toe to toe with him any day and I'll be damned if I'm the one to back down. While this eased her fears a little, I made sure to take her mind off it completely by burying my head between her legs.

Come Monday, I didn't want to return to work. I'd rather stay in bed with her, but I need to get this control arm finished. The car is up on the lift while I work underneath. With my arms above me, I tighten a bolt when two pairs of legs catch my attention. When Jay calls my name, I drop my arms and step out from beneath the car. Standing next to Jay is a guy I never expected to see in my shop. I eye him up and down, wary of why he's here.

Jay's glance shifts between the two of us before he nervously reverses his steps. "I'll let you two talk." Jay turns and walks to the other side of the garage, leaving us alone.

To be polite, I hold out my hand for him to shake, but he only glares at it as if I might give him cooties. I shrug it off. So that's how this is going to be.

I mimic his stance and cross my arms over my chest. Man to man. Neither of us backing down. "What can I help you with today?"

"I'm not here for any bullshit, so I'll get to the point. My family has always been my top priority—"

"And let me guess, me being with Olivia is a problem?"

"I'm looking out for her best interest."

"The way I see it, you're looking out for *your* best interest."

"My interest is her best interest."

I drop my hands and take a step closer to him. "Olivia's a grown adult. She can make her own decisions, and I won't let her father scare me away. If she doesn't want to be with me, she'll have to tell me herself."

He glances around my shop before meeting my gaze and squaring his shoulders. "You've got a nice shop here. I'd hate to see something happen and you lose it."

I huff out a laugh. "Are you threatening me?"

"All I'm saying is it would be best if you no longer see my daughter. I know all about your past, and I won't let you tarnish her reputation."

"You don't know shit about me or my past. Either way, Olivia knows me. And she has chosen to be with me."

He takes a step closer and leans in. "Unfortunately, you think you know my daughter. The only thing she cares about is what I put in her bank account. She's led a very easy life and I know she won't give all that up to be with someone who doesn't reach her standards. Like I said, it's best if you just let her go before she gets hurt."

I scoff. "I'm not scared of you or your empty threats."

"Fine, then." He retreats and reaches for the inside pocket of his suit jacket and holds out a piece of paper. When I stare at it, he nods for me to take it. I snatch it from his grasp and slowly unfold the paper. "It's a check for ten-thousand dollars. It's all yours. Maybe you buy yourself some new tools for your shop. But stay away from my daughter."

I stare down at the five digits written in pen. I won't lie, I could find a lot of use for this money. But that's not me. I don't take threats. I don't take bribes. "Now it's my turn to say something. It would be in your best interest to get the fuck out of my shop." I hold the check out in front of me and rip it in half, tossing the two pieces of paper in his face until they flutter to the ground.

He narrows his eyes at me as we have a stare off. There's no way I'm backing down. If we were in the Wild West, it would be a draw on who would pull their pistol from their holster first. Finally, he turns on his heel and storms out the open overhead door. *Bang. Bang.* I clench and unclench my fists at my side. Who does he think he is? Coming in here and demanding anything from me.

A few minutes later, Jay steps up next to me. "What was that about?"

"Olivia's dad coming here with empty threats and trying to bribe me to stay away from her. He doesn't like the big, bad biker with his daughter."

Jay reaches down and picks up the two pieces of paper and holds them together. "Damn. That's all? You'd figure his daughter would be worth more than that."

"He's a piece of shit." I grab the pieces of paper from him and shove them in my pocket. This is one thing I can't keep secret from Olivia.

## CHAPTER THIRTY-THREE

# CUTTING TIES

*Olivia*

Nothing is worse than having to sit at your desk all day, turned on, because the highlight reel of the weekend plays on repeat in your head. All I want to do is text Ledger and have a lunch break sexting session, but he told me he had a big job he needed to finish today. But after work, it's game on. Or sex on is more like it.

My phone buzzes on the desk next to me. My heart skips a beat. Maybe he finished early.

LEDGER

Your dad just paid me a visit at my shop.

My jaw hits the desk. What the hell was my dad doing visiting Ledger?

OLIVIA

What did he want?

LEDGER

Told me to stay away from you.

My heart stops. I can't believe he would do this. No, wait. I can. More importantly, what did Ledger say? A giant lump forms in my throat as I watch the three dots bounce as he types.

LEDGER

He bribed me with a check for 10k.

Next, a picture of the torn check comes through. I exhale a sigh of relief.

LEDGER

Fuck his money.

OLIVIA

I could kiss you right now.

OLIVIA

But also, wtf? There has to be some misunderstanding.

My phone pings again, but this time it isn't Ledger. It's my father.

DAD

Stop by the house after work. We need to talk.

Why does that sound so ominous?

OLIVIA

I just got a message from my dad. He wants me to go to the house after work. I'll ask what all this is about.

Once I'm finished with work, I head to my parents' house. When I pull up to the closed gate, I punch in the code and the wrought iron gates open. As I snake up the driveway the expansive house comes into view through the trees. I park my SUV in front of the closed garage. I pluck my purse off the passenger seat and make my way to the front door. Twisting the knob, I let myself in. Hushed murmurs can be heard in the kitchen, so I follow the voices down the hallway to the arched doorway. My mom sits at the kitchen island with a folder and papers strewn out in front of her while my dad stands on the other side. I approach the situation cautiously with the information about paying Ledger off tucked in my back pocket. I want to know what they have to say first.

"Hey everyone. What's going on?" Both their heads turn to me. Their faces are not warm and inviting. I slow my pace as a ball of anxiety settles in my stomach.

My dad glares at me. "What do you have to say for yourself?"

"If I knew what you were talking about, I might be able to answer."

He grabs a couple of papers in front of my mom and pushes them toward me.

"Explain yourself." He glowers.

I flip the papers over and pictures of me and Ledger at the lake come into view. The pictures I had him take of me on his bike. My heart drops to the floor like a lead weight. With trembling fingers, I flip through page after page of printed photos.

"These are all over the internet. Everyone now knows the senator's daughter is a whore," he spits.

I flinch at his words. "How did you get these?" My voice is shaky.

"On the internet. They're out in the public for everyone to see. When I had the IP address tracked, guess who it belonged to?" My gaze shoots to my dad. "Your tattooed boy toy. Can't you see he's using you? I'm sure he's raking in the big bucks selling these online, especially to my campaign challengers."

There is no way Ledger would post these. He wouldn't do that. Deep down, I know he wouldn't. Hell, he didn't want to take the photos. I convinced him to do it. "You're lying."

He slides another piece of paper toward me. I peer down at the black ink showing a string of numbers with Ledger's name and his internet service provider. He rests his palms on the counter and leans in, trying to intimidate me. "Now, I'm lying? Do you not realize how damaging this is to our family? To my career?" He slams his fist on the island and I jump. "I can't believe you'd be so selfish. That you'd trust a degenerate over your blood family. You're mother tried to set you up with a good man from a good family and this is how you repay us?" He picks up a couple of the printed photos and tosses them at me. They float down to the counter, a couple of them falling to the floor.

I scoff. "We may be blood, but that's the only thing that connects us. Ledger has been in my life for only two months, and in that short time he's been there for me, supporting me way more than you have in thirty-one years. So yes, I'm going to trust him a hundred times out of ten."

"You think he's going to take care of you? I guarantee he can't afford your tastes."

"He's shown me what love is! Not the fake façade you've given me!"

"The way I see it, he's done enough damage to this family. The only way to fix it is to stop seeing him."

"Is that why you showed up at his shop today and attempted to bribe him to stay away? Why don't you want me to be happy? Because I don't want to live my life as miserable as you two." I snap my gaze between my parents.

"If he knew what was good for him, he would have taken the money. Instead, he left me no other choice. Either you break up with him and never see him again, or be with him and no longer be a part of this family."

"You can't be serious? An ultimatum?" My gaze shifts to my mom. "Mom? This can't be real."

She looks away, unable to look me in the eye. I knew my mom had no backbone, but this takes it to an all-new level.

"If you're forcing me to choose, I will always pick Ledger. You know why? He would never do this to me!"

"I hope he can afford your expensive tastes because you're cut off. Your credit card? Done. Your bills? Everything is now your responsibility. You have one week to remove all your belongings from the house before I change the locks."

My face flames red hot. I can't believe he's doing this to his own daughter, and for what? Dating a guy he doesn't approve of? Being happy? If that's the case, I don't want to be here. Yanking out my wallet, I chuck my black card his way, hitting him in the arm. "I don't need it. I don't need any of it. Most of all, I don't need you." I turn to my mom, who still can't look at me. "You want to live this life, fine. But not me. I know what I want, and I won't let you, either of you, take that away from me."

I storm down the hallway and slam the front door behind me. Somehow, I've held it together, but once I'm a quarter mile down the road, everything hits me at once. Like a semi-truck barreling down the road at sixty miles per hour. My vision blurs from the tears pooling in my eyes. I slam on the brakes and pull off onto the dirt shoulder. A cloud of dust floats behind me.

I can't believe that happened. All of it. I know Ledger doesn't exactly fit into my world, but why does it matter? I love him. I. Love. Him. Pulling down the visor, I use the mirror and wipe away the moisture. Once I'm situated, I shove the shifter into drive and stomp on the gas with only one destination in mind.

# CHAPTER THIRTY-FOUR

# PERMANENT SLEEPOVERS

*Ledger*

I'm standing at my counter, squirting mustard onto a slice of bread, and then another. Grabbing the slice without the salami, I plop it on top of the other and smash it down. With both hands I lift the sandwich to my mouth when a light knock sounds on my door. I freeze.

The rapping starts again.

I drop my sandwich to the counter, stroll to the door, and pull it open. Her eyes are puffy and bloodshot. Something happened. The urge to kill someone is strong.

"Can I come in?" Her voice is soft and quiet, the opposite of her normal, cheerful self.

Pulling the door open farther, I step to the side, and she slides past me before turning around.

"My life is a mess." Her gaze falls to the floor.

I've never seen her this defeated. Normally, she's the one doing everything to make me smile and right now my heart hurts that she can't smile herself. I hate seeing her like this. My jaw clenches, and I want to burn down the entire city just to get to whoever hurt her.

Stepping backward, I take a seat on a barstool at the counter. I reach for her wrists and pull her in between my spread legs. "Who do I have to kill?"

Her lips twist into a weak smile. "How do you feel about having a homeless girlfriend?"

"What are you talking about?" I run my hands up and down her arms.

Her fingers twist into knots between us. "Where do I start?" She exhales a deep breath.

I give her all the time she needs to collect her thoughts.

"After you told me about the check, I got a message from my parents wanting me to meet them at their house. As soon as I got there, I knew something was wrong. Then he showed me pictures from our day at the lake. Apparently, somehow, they ended up on the internet—"

"What the fuck? I never did that."

"I know. I know you would never do something like that. But I don't know how they got there. Anyway, after I confronted him about the check, he said if you were smart you would have taken the money. Then he gave me an ultimatum. My family or you. I chose the only thing that makes me happy." Her gaze meets mine. "You."

I run my hands over her hips and around to her ass. With my hands splayed out over the denim, I pull her closer to me. "I will fight the world to make you happy." I press a kiss to her lips. Pulling away but close enough that we're still slightly touching, I say, "I don't have a homeless girlfriend." I pause. "Move in with me."

Her eyes flutter open. "Wait? Are you serious?"

"You'd never survive on the streets." I shrug a shoulder.

"You're not wrong. But are you sure?"

"This is what you get. It's nothing fancy with marble floors and appliances that wipe your ass."

She chuckles.

"But this is what I got."

Her gaze slowly meets mine. "It's perfect. Anywhere you are is perfect. It'll be like a permanent sleepover." She throws her arms around my neck and presses her body into mine. After a moment, she pulls away. "I hate to ruin this happy moment, but what do we do about my father? I don't know if he's going to try and do anything or not."

I wrap my arms around her waist, holding her tight to reassure her I'm not letting her go. "He's gotta torch the entire city before he can even try to split us up." She gives me a small smile and nods in understanding. I nuzzle the crook of her neck, inhaling her sweet jasmine scent. I press gentle kisses to her warm skin as I hold her. Years have passed since I've been emotionally invested in another woman. She's the complete opposite of me, but when we are together, we're a force to be reckoned with.

"I don't know what I would do without you. I love you." We both freeze as soon as those three words fall from her lips. "I. Um. I—"

Before she can finish her sentence, I lift my hand and grip her chin, not wanting to give her a chance to rescind her words. To tell me that she didn't mean it. "I love you. Fuck. I'm pretty sure I've been in love with you since you stormed into my life and demanded that I kiss you."

The blue in her eyes sparkles like I've never seen before. Her lips pull into a smile. "I generally get what I want." She shrugs playfully. "But in all seriousness, we're doing this? Living together?"

"We're doing this duchess. I love you so damn much."

235

My fingers run along her temple, tucking a strand of hair behind her ear.

"I love you, too." She pauses. "But we may have a problem, though." She sucks the corner of her bottom lip into her mouth.

"What's that?" I run my thumb along her lip, pulling it from her grasp.

"Your closet isn't going to be big enough to hold all my clothes." Her nose scrunches up.

I bark out a laugh. "We'll figure something out. Can't have your clothes going homeless."

"Thank you so much. This means so much to me." She cups my cheeks. Her fingers brush across my stubble.

"We could celebrate?" I wiggle my eyebrows.

"Yes! Should we go out somewhere? Or maybe order takeout?"

"Or more along the lines of eating your pussy as an appetizer and then for the main course, stuffing you full of my cock." I grip her hips and haul her closer to me, my bulge pressing directly into her sex.

"Mmm. I like your idea of celebrating much better. Then, for dessert, I can suck you dry."

"What are we waiting for? Our bed for two awaits." With my arms wrapped around her, I rise to my feet, causing her to take a step backward. Then I lift her while she wraps her legs around my waist with a giggle. She cups my cheeks and presses her lips to mine as I blindly navigate us to my—our—bedroom.

The next morning, I stir awake after a night filled with her screaming my name. My girl is insatiable, but I'll give her whatever she wants. Speaking of which, I roll over to wrap her up in my arms when I'm met with a cold, empty bed. All of a sudden, the banging of metal draws my attention. I roll off the edge as a cool rush of air hits my naked body. On the floor next to her dress, I find a pair of gray sweatpants and tug them on. The noise gets louder as I stroll into the kitchen. As I enter, I come to a halt and prop myself against the door frame. Over the next few seconds, I admire Olivia as she moves around my kitchen. Jack circles her feet, moving in one leg and then out the other. She reaches up to one of the cupboards. The hem of my shirt she's wearing rides up, exposing the soft flesh of her backside.

"Morning, duchess."

She fumbles with the coffee mugs in her hand, almost dropping them. She sets them on the counter and whirls around. "Oh shit. You scared me."

I push off the door frame and stroll toward her. Her gaze wanders over my chest and down to my sweatpants, then back up. When I reach her, I rest one hand on one counter while the other is on the island, blocking her path.

"I love waking up like this."

"Me making you breakfast?"

"No. You wearing my shirt. Breakfast is just a bonus."

She beams up at me and steps into my space, wrapping her arms around my neck. "Lucky for you, you get both."

Not wanting to let her go, I wrap my arms tighter around her waist. "How about later, we get all your things? We can use my truck and I'll recruit Jay to help as well."

"That would be fantastic. I'll call my friends. The couple of suitcases I have won't last me much longer."

"So you're telling me you'll have nothing to wear? Maybe we should wait a few more days?" I wink.

# CHAPTER THIRTY-FIVE

# THE TOY BOX

## Olivia

Three truck loads later, everything is moved into Ledger's house. Everyone left once we got all the boxes inside. I'll work on organizing and putting everything away later. Sweat trickles down my temple and I wipe it away with the back of my hand. Never in my wildest dreams did I think I would have to move out of my house, but I didn't want to live by their rules anymore. It's now time to live for me. Every butterfly needs to eventually break out of the cocoon, spread their wings, and fly away. I know I won't have to do it alone. Ledger will be by my side.

His nose must have itched because at that moment, Ledger strolls into the bedroom and drops a box onto the bed. "This one piqued my interest." He stares at the box marked *Toys* and swings his gaze to mine. A sly smile appears on his face.

Heat creeps up my neck. Before I can say anything, he's pulling apart the top flaps and peeks inside before pouring the contents onto the bed. A variety of dildos, vibrators, lube, and a jeweled butt plug tumble on to the duvet cover.

"Well, well, my good girl isn't as good as I thought." He quirks an eyebrow.

"A girl has needs and sometimes she needs to take matters into her own hands." I start to collect all my toys, but his fingers wrap around my wrist, stopping me. Then he pulls me to his chest.

"Not anymore. All your orgasms are now mine." His hand trails up my back until his fingers wrap around the nape of my neck. "The rest of the unpacking can wait. I want to play, starting with this silver one." Before I can say anything, his lips crash to mine in a bruising kiss. The tips of his fingers bite into the base of my neck.

I can't fight the needy moan that escapes. I love that he doesn't treat me like delicate crystal. Until him, I never knew I liked a little pain with my pleasure. But with Ledger, it's become something I crave.

He twists us around, so I'm lying on the bed, and breaks our kiss. Heat and desire swirls in his irises. I know mine are the same. His hands grip my waist and he tosses me onto the bed and I can't help but squeal in surprise. The dildos and vibrators bounce from my weight. Ledger crawls up the bed, eyes a stormy gray as if he's stalking his prey. I'll let him catch me every single time.

He props himself up on his elbows, careful to not put all his weight on me as he nestles between my spread legs. The tip of his nose brushes across my neck as his stubble scrapes across my overly sensitive skin. My nipples pebble in anticipation for what's coming.

When his lips reach my ear, he whispers, "Duchess, you're mine. This body is mine. Now, I'm going to take what's mine."

"Yes. I'm all yours." I buck my hips, hoping to find any sort of friction. His bulge rubs against my clit through my thin yoga pants. A needy moan escapes me.

He trails kisses across my jaw until he meets my lips in a bruising kiss. Hard and demanding. My fingers tangle in the hair at the back of his head, and I hold him to me, relishing in the feel of him everywhere. All my senses are on high alert. Wanting to smell his masculine sandalwood scent, to hearing his moans and grunts, to feeling him on every inch of my body, to seeing the lust and desire in his eyes. His tongue presses at the seam of my lips, seeking entrance, and I open up for him. Our tongues stroke and caress each other's. His hand skates up my body until he's cupping my breast, kneading the soft flesh. I whimper and writhe underneath him.

He breaks away. "Your body is so needy for me." His words are a whisper across my lips. He moves his hand down to the hem of my shirt and lifts it up over my bra. Goosebumps cover my skin when it comes in contact with the cool air. He presses open mouth kisses down my chest and between my breasts, taking turns sucking and biting on the right and then the left. The sting of pain causes me to moan louder.

"Ledger. I. Need. You." My words come out in breathy pants.

"Patience. You'll love what I have in store for you." His finger digs into the cup of my bra and pulls down, my hard nipple springing out. I thrust up, needing more of him. All of him. "My girl's needy."

"Please. Ledger." I moan when his lips trap my nipple, swirling his tongue around the stiff peak.

"Are you wet for me?"

"So wet." I arch my back off the bed, pressing my chest farther into him.

"I don't know. I'll have to see for myself." His hand skims down my torso until he reaches the waistband of my black yoga pants and slips inside. His fingertips trail down my silk panties. I spread my legs wider as he circles my clit over the fabric.

"Ah! Yes!"

"You're soaked through your panties." He pushes them to the side and runs his finger down my slit.

A shiver runs through my body as soon as he touches my clit. The simplest touch setting my body ablaze. I release a needy moan. He plunges a finger into my pussy, pumping in and out before adding a second.

"Always so needy for me." He uses his other hand to pull down my yoga pants. I lift my hips to help him as he slides them down my legs. Then he does the same with my panties, all the while still leisurely fingering me. With his free hand, he spreads me open. "Look at that pretty pussy. Just begging me to lick it clean."

"Oh, Ledger! Please!"

"Only because you asked nicely." He climbs off the end of the bed and drags me by the ankles so I'm at the edge. Lowering himself to the floor, he runs the tip of his tongue up my center and then flicks my clit. My body jolts from the contact but soon my moans fill the room. With the flat of his tongue, he continues to lap at my wetness. I whimper every time he reaches my clit. This spurs him on more, driving me closer and closer to the edge with every lick. "You taste sweet like honey. I could lick your pussy all day." I squirm from his words. He pulls his fingers out, and a whine escapes me from the loss.

Suddenly, the tip of something cold runs through my wetness. I prop myself up on my elbows and notice the glint of a silver vibrator. My teeth sink into my bottom lip when Ledger's gaze meets mine through his eyelashes. Slowly, he sinks it into my opening. I arch my back in pleasure, causing the vibrator to go deeper. I've never had anyone use a vibrator on me before. Something about it is so intimate and hot. He glances down and watches as it disappears inside me.

"Keep going. That feels so good." My breathy moans turn into breathless pants.

Ledger continues to thrust the vibrator in and out of me, fast and hard. His lips wrap around my clit and sucks. My fingers claw at the comforter as the sensation sends me over the edge. Stars burst behind my eyelids and my orgasm takes over, sending a blissful chill coursing through my body. I moan out Ledger's name and he slows the pace to leisurely strokes, then he pulls the vibrator out.

He sits up, ushering me backward as he crawls up my body and presses his mouth to mine. I can taste myself on his lips, but I don't care. There's something hot and carnal about the way he can ravish my body. With his lips still on mine, he sits me upright, his hand wraps around me and in one flick, my bra comes undone. He pulls my shirt over my head and tosses it to the ground. The straps of my bra fall off my shoulders and he drags them the rest of the way off and throws it toward my shirt.

His gaze wanders over my naked body, appreciating everything in his sight. Then his eyes meet mine. "Undress me."

I don't need to be told twice. He moves so he's standing at the end of the bed. Rising up, I scoot so I'm sitting in front of him, my hands slide under the hem of his shirt and I run them up his torso. My breathing increases as I caress every dip and valley of his abs. I shift myself so I'm on my knees, then I continue to drag my hands over his hard chest. He lifts his arms and I pull his shirt over his head with assistance from him. On my way down, I caress his chest again, admiring all his tattoos. Stories of his life in art form. I glance at him through my eyelashes, his hooded eyes watch my every move, encouraging me to continue. When I reach the belt buckle, I pull the leather from the latch and let it fall open. My fingers pop open the button and dip into the waistband of his jeans. I slide my hands inside and pull both his jeans and his boxer briefs down. His cock springs free and juts out. My tongue peeks out, wetting my lips. A bead of pre-cum sits on the tip. I bend down and wrap my lips around the tip and suck. A throaty groan leaves him. I swirl my tongue around his head, giving extra attention to the silver ball on the end. Ledger's fingers thread into the hair at the base of my head and he thrusts his hips, causing me to take him deeper. He continues to tunnel himself in and out of my mouth. I bring a hand up and massage his balls.

"Ah! Fuck! Your mouth is fucking perfection. Sucking me down like a good girl." He picks up his speed, hitting the back of my throat on every thrust, and I fight not to gag around him. And then he's pulling out. "As much as I want you to swallow me down, I want to be inside you when I come. Get on your hands and knees."

I do as he says and wiggle my ass at him.

"Duchess, are you tempting me?"

I glance over my shoulder. "Is it working?"

*Crack.* His hand connects with my ass cheek, and I yelp.

"Never tempt a starving man." He rubs his hand over the stinging flesh and this time I moan. He runs his thumb over my puckered hole. "I want to fuck you here." At his words, he applies the slightest pressure with his thumb, and I gasp. "Not today. We'll work you up to taking my cock."

The bed dips when he reaches over and grabs a bottle of lube. He squirts a little on my crack and the cool liquid slides down. With his thumb he rubs it around the tight muscle, making sure it's coated. While he does that, he grabs the silver vibrator. "We'll start with this." He shoves it into my pussy, and I moan. The double sensation of the vibrator and his thumb is overwhelming, but I don't want it to stop. With every thrust, I push back against him. He pulls the vibrator out and I whimper. Then the warm, wet tip is at my other hole. The click of the lube top opening sounds, I glance over my shoulder, and he's squirting some on to the vibrator then tosses the bottle to the side.

Slowly, he pushes the tip into me. I inhale a sharp breath. "Relax for me, duchess." I exhale through my mouth, opening myself up to him. Inch by inch he pushes it deeper into me. I pinch my eyes closed at the strange intrusion. "Such a good girl, taking all the vibrator. Getting herself ready to take my cock."

His words turn me on, and I push against the vibrator, sinking down farther. It's a foreign feeling, but one I'm growing to enjoy. With it still in me, Ledger runs his fingers through my pussy and rubs circles around my clit. From his touch, I forget all about the vibrator.

"That's it duchess. Doesn't it feel good?"

"Yes! So good."

"I'm going to move the vibrator now. Just enjoy the feeling."

All I can do is nod. He pulls it out, but not all the way and then pushes it back in, all the while still rubbing my clit. My teeth sink into my bottom lip, the pleasure mixing with the slight sting of pain as he plunges the vibrator in and out faster. A tingle shoots up my legs as my toes curl, hitting me right in my core. My pants and moans fill the room as my orgasm bursts though me like a white hot explosion. My head falls to the mattress as I collect my breath. I've felt nothing like that before, and fuck, it felt so good.

"Fuck. You look so hot with this vibrator in your ass. I'll keep it there while I fuck you."

I gasp when he rubs the tip of his cock at my entrance. Once the head is inside, he plunges into me. I let out a cross between a moan and a scream. "Oh God! I feel so full."

He pulls out and thrusts back in. Before I can catch my breath, he's doing it again and again. The silver ball at the tip of his cock, runs along my inner wall. The head hitting my g-spot on every thrust. Another orgasm is on the brink of bursting through me. Ledger tugs on the vibrator and shoves it back into me with shallow thrusts while his cock impales my pussy. The double stimulation is almost too much. My heavy pants turn into screams of pleasure. His grunts become louder and faster. My pussy clenches around him as another orgasm takes hold. Ledger's soon follows as his hot cum shoots inside me.

# CHAPTER THIRTY-SIX

# UNLOCKING MY HEART

*Ledger*

"Holy shit." I still inside her.

She tosses her blonde hair to the side and peers over her shoulder at me. "I've never felt anything like that, ever. I'm pretty sure I saw stars. Literal stars sparkled behind my lids."

"We're definitely doing that again."

The twinkle in her eyes tells me she wants that too. I ease out of her and playfully smack her ass. "Hold tight. I'll be right back."

As soon as I saw the box in her things, I had a sneaking suspicion of what was inside. Sure enough, I was right, and the opportunity wasn't going to pass me up. The best part, Olivia was just as eager as me. She surprises me more and more every day.

I climb off the bed and make my way out of the bedroom and into the bathroom. Tugging a washcloth off the pile from the shelf, I run it under warm water. Once I return to the bedroom, I run the cloth between her legs, cleaning her up. When I'm done, I toss it to the corner of the room, landing next to the dirty laundry basket. She rolls over and climbs off the bed.

"Where are you going?" I wrap an arm around her chest and haul her to lie down next to me on the bed. I tug a small blanket over us, and I hold her in my arms.

"You're initiating a cuddle?" She nuzzles into the crook of my arm.

"This is just my resting position."

"Or you wanted to cuddle?" Her hand splays over my chest.

I trail my fingers up and down her forearm. "Fine. Only because it's with you. Don't tell anyone. I'll deny it."

Her shoulders bounce with laughter. She turns toward me, resting her chin on my chest. "Your secret is safe with me." She runs a finger over one of my tattoos, tracing the outline of a feather. "Any plans for more tattoos?"

"I have an idea, but it's not quite perfect yet."

"What is it?"

"It's a secret." The corner of my lips turn up into a sly smile.

She bats her eyelashes. "Please?"

"The begging only works when I'm between your legs."

She laughs. And it's my second favorite sound. The first is when she chants my name. "Have you thought of getting a tattoo? Your flawless skin could use some ink."

She tilts her head to the side, scrunching her nose as she thinks. "Not really. My parents always told me to never defile my body. No tattoos. No piercings, besides my ears. Even then it could only be my lobes. I remember my mom went into this whole spiel about tattoos are forever and what will happen when I get older."

"You could have gotten something that's concealed so they would never know." I run a finger down her chest, between her tits. "Like here." I continue to move my hand south, over her hips to cup one ass cheek. "Or here."

"My ass?" A sexy smile graces her lips.

I wiggle my eyebrows in response.

"Even if it's hidden, they would find out somehow. Someone would see me walk into the tattoo parlor or something." Her gaze falls to my chest.

"Since you're living on the edge now, dating the bad boy, might as well do something bad. Would you want to get one?" Her nose scrunches again, and fuck, she's so cute.

"I don't know what I would get."

"I have an idea."

"What's that?"

Throwing the blanket off me, I roll out of bed. I pick up my boxer briefs and tug them on. Olivia's eyebrows pinch together as she watches me warily. When I reach my dresser, I pull open the top drawer and dig to the bottom until I find a folded piece of paper. I had this drawn up twelve years ago, the same time I got the padlock tattoo that covers my heart. I wasn't sure if I'd ever give it to someone, but Olivia has branded herself on me and into my life. Deep in my soul, I know this is meant to be.

Closing the drawer, I make my way back to the bed and sit down, resting against the headboard. She sits up next to me, mimicking my pose. She lifts the blanket to cover herself.

"What's on the paper?"

I inhale a deep breath. Being vulnerable is not my thing. In fact, I do everything in my power so I'm not in that position. But this feels right. Olivia feels right. I hold out the piece of paper toward her. She peers at it, then me, and I nod for her to take it. Slowly, she plucks the white paper from my grasp, still unsure of what it could be. She peels the corner of the paper open, unfolding it.

Her head tilts to the side. "A skeleton key?"

"It is but take a closer look. What's the key for?"

She inspects the paper closer, memorizing the intricate vine design. Her eyes go wide when recognition hits. She turns toward me and presses the paper just below my heart, under the padlock. "This is the key to your lock," she whispers.

"It is. And I want you to have it." I grip her chin, forcing her eyes to meet mine. "I never imagined I would meet a woman who would make me feel alive again. I love you. And I want you to have the key to my heart."

Moisture pools in the corners of her eyes. "Ledger. I don't know what to say. I love you. So much. You challenged me to step outside my bubble and experience life in a whole new way. I could have never done that without you." She lifts the blanket and moves to straddle my lap. Her warm hands cup my cheeks and she presses her lips to mine. It's a kiss full of love and unspoken promises.

Breaking the kiss, my gaze meets hers. "So, what do you say, want to get a tattoo?"

"Yes. Yes. A million times, yes." She kisses me again. When she pulls away, she peers down at the paper. "Where should I get it?"

"Wherever you want. Just knowing you have it is all I need."

Her nose scrunches. Several seconds pass before her eyes meet mine. "I know where I want it."

"Where?"

"It's a secret."

I bark out a laugh. "Touché"

"So, when can we go?"

"I'll call my guy and set up an appointment." I run my hands up her sides, her smooth skin under my fingers.

"But first we should celebrate," she says, a devilish glint in her eyes.

"My kind of celebrating or yours?"

"We'll go with yours." She wraps her arms around my neck and kisses me. I hold her to me and roll us over.

After I called my tattoo artist, he pulled some strings for me and got Olivia in the next day. We walk hand in hand into the shop. I've never been one for public displays of affection, but in this case, I want everyone to know she's mine.

Excitedly, she tugs me up to the counter.

The purple-haired receptionist, Cora, glances up. "Hey Ledger. Ryke mentioned you have an appointment today." She digs around for some paperwork. She's been here for as long as I've come here.

"Not for me, but for my girlfriend," I peer down at her, unable to fight my smile, "Olivia."

"Fantastic. I'll just need you to sign these." She pushes a form toward us.

Ryke enters the reception area from a hallway next to the desk. "Ledger. Good to see you, man." His hand extends toward me.

I clasp his hand in mine and give it a shake. "Same to you. This is my girlfriend, Olivia."

"Hi, nice to meet you." She holds out her hand.

Ryke leans in toward me and whispers, "You're one lucky son of a bitch."

Olivia links her arms with mine. "I'm actually the lucky one." She winks at Ryke.

He releases a low whistle. "Don't let this one go." He props an elbow on the counter. "So, I understand you already know what you want." Ryke's gaze dances between mine and Olivia's.

"Yes." Olivia excitedly pulls out the sketch from her pocket and hands it over to Ryke.

He peels the side of the paper open. Tilting his head, he studies the drawing. "This looks familiar." His gaze shoots to mine. "If I remember correctly, I drew this one for you. What, ten years ago?"

"Twelve," I say.

"Well, let's get to it. Don't want this one chickening out." He winks at Olivia, then he guides us down the hallway to an open area with tattoo chairs. When Olivia enters, Ryke stops me by clasping my shoulder. "Congrats, man. I know what this tattoo means to you."

With that, he turns and rubs his hands together. "So, where's this tattoo going? Do we need a private room?"

"Private room?" She blinks rapidly before her gaze slingshots to mine, wanting an answer.

"Do you need to take any clothes off for where you want the tattoo?"

"Oh!" Her eyes go wide. "No. No private room is needed."

"Where am I putting the tattoo?"

Olivia holds up her right hand. "On my wrist." Ryke guides her to take a seat in a black, leather tattoo chair. He then gets to work tracing the skeleton key design onto transfer paper.

I pull up a stool on her left side so I can be with her for

her first time. She stretches out her hand to me. I intertwine my fingers with hers and softly rub the pad of my thumb over the soft skin of her palm.

"What was that with Ryke? A man moment?"

I laugh. "Something like that." Bending down, I place a kiss on her wrist.

A few minutes later, Ryke returns and stretches on a pair of black latex gloves. He tells her everything he's going to do as he preps the area. He asks her which direction she wants the tattoo to face, and she tells him. The buzzing of the tattoo gun fires up, the only sound in the room. On the first touch of the gun to her skin, Olivia pinches her eyes closed and flings her head toward me. She inhales a sharp breath through her nose and then slowly lets it out. A few seconds later, she slowly opens her eyes, meeting mine.

"You got this, duchess. I'm here for you."

All she does is nod her head.

Over the next thirty minutes, I continue to hold her hand. When the pain subsides and she relaxes, she sneaks glances at Ryke's work as it comes together. Every swirl, every line connecting to make the perfect piece of art. Something my girl will have with her forever. She'll have a piece of me forever.

When Ryke is finished, he pushes his stool away. "You're all done."

She lifts her arm to inspect her wrist. The shape of a skeleton key is outlined in red. "Oh my God. I love it," she whispers.

Both of us admire the mostly black tattoo with areas of shading. At the bow are three circles connected by half swirls on the side, along with a few other decorative design elements. At the beginning of the shank is another circle, and at the end is the bit with three notches.

"Did it hurt?"

"At first it was startling, but eventually I got used to it."

"I have to ask, why your right wrist?"

She smiles, soft and sweet. "So, whenever I press my palm to your heart, I'm unlocking it."

"You and me against the world. Together, we're unstoppable." My words are quiet so only she can hear. She mouths "I love you."

Just then, Ryke reappears with some ointment and a wrap for her new ink. After he's finished with her aftercare and providing direction for what she needs to do at home, I grip her other hand, intertwining my fingers with hers. "Let's go home." Our home. And fuck, it feels good to say that.

## CHAPTER THIRTY-SEVEN

# EXORCISE A FEW DEMONS

*Olivia*

My eyes flutter open and I attempt to stretch my arms, but I'm pinned to the mattress. A big arm inked with colorful artwork is draped over my chest just below my breasts. A slow smile graces my lips. It's been over a week since I've moved in with Ledger. I love seeing my things mixed with his, but most of all, I love waking up in his arms every morning. As if he knows I'm thinking about him, he pulls me closer.

*I think he likes it too.*

You'd never guess a thirty-one-year-old has never cohabitated with a guy before, but I always had my own house. And I very much enjoyed having my own space, so the desire to share with anyone didn't exist. Until now. They say everything happens for a reason. Taking the seat next to Ledger, kissing him, and falling head over stilettos in love with him is my reason.

With his arm still draped over me, I roll to my side to face him. My movements cause him to stir awake. Hooded, deep, steely gray eyes meet mine. "Good morning."

"Good morning, beautiful." His voice is low and gravelly from sleep. "How long were you watching me sleep?"

"Oh, not too long. Hour tops." I bite back my laughter.

"Next time, I'll have to give you something worthwhile to watch." He pulls me tighter to him. His hard cock pressing into my stomach.

"Is that so?" I run my fingers over his chest, faintly tracing his tattoos, which has become a favorite pastime of mine. Pretty soon, I'm going to have them all memorized.

He rolls us over so I'm now straddling his hips. Only two thin layers of fabric keep him from slipping inside me. I rest my palms on his chest, my right one covering his padlock tattoo, while he runs his fingers up and down my thighs. Without realizing it, I slowly grind myself up and down his length.

"Fuck, duchess." He groans, almost painfully. "Don't start something you don't intend to finish."

"No worries. I fully intend on finishing. All over your cock."

He moves his hand down, so it's between us, and moves my panties to the side. I inhale a sharp breath as I easily slide down his thick length, stretching me in by inch.

"Look how your tight pussy wraps around my dick. Sucking me in." He bucks his hips, pushing deeper into me, the silver ball hitting my g-spot and I'm already on the brink of orgasm. "That's it duchess. Take what you want. Ride my cock."

His words spur me on to move faster and faster. My

pants and moans grow louder, echoing off the surrounding walls. I'm pretty sure any person walking by can hear me chanting Ledger's name from inside. My toes curl and I dig my nails into his muscular chest as my orgasm crashes through me fast and furious. Ledger groans, bucking his hips into me, chasing his own orgasm. Seconds later, his hot seed spills inside me. Both of us breathless, our hearts racing as we float back down to Earth. I lean forward and rest my cheek on his chest. He wraps his arms around me, holding me close.

"New rule. We start off every morning like this." He trails his hands up and down the cotton covering my back. His cotton shirt.

"You're insatiable."

"Only when it comes to you. But also, you just know it's going to be a good day when it starts off with an orgasm."

"It's hard to argue with that." I press a kiss to his chest. The same spot I had my head on moments ago. I rise off him and exit the bedroom to get cleaned up in the bathroom. When I return, Ledger's dressed and typing on his phone, a scowl covering his face. "What's wrong?"

He places his phone on the dresser. "Jay said a package was dropped off at the shop. No address, just my name."

"That's odd." Just then, my phone buzzes on the nightstand. Glancing down, my sister's name pops up with the text. I type out a quick reply. "Tatum wants me to meet her for lunch."

"Okay. I'm going to head out to the shop and see what this package is."

"Be careful. Open it slowly in case it's a glitter bomb." I motion my hands like a bomb exploding. "Glitter everywhere. You'd sparkle for days."

"Thanks. I'll keep that in mind." He grips the nape of

my neck and hauls me to him, pressing his lips to mine. "Enjoy lunch with your sister." After one last peck, he releases me and makes his way out of the bedroom, and then the bathroom door clicks shut.

I walk to the half open bi-fold doors and rifle through the cramped closet. By the time I find an outfit and make my way to the bathroom to take a shower, Ledger is long gone. An hour later, I'm ready and head out to meet Tatum.

I pull into the parking lot of a small café. As I climb out of my SUV, my phone buzzes with a text from my sister, letting me know she already has a table. I sling my purse over my shoulder and tug my cream colored, oversized, cable knit cardigan tighter around me as the breeze flutters around me. When I enter the large wood double doors of the café, I inform the hostess I'm meeting my party here. She guides me into the large dining room. Tables draped in white tablecloths are strategically placed throughout the open room. The afternoon sun beams through the large floor to ceiling windows, casting a glimmering reflection of Lake Superior.

I round a pillar and freeze. With slow, cautious footsteps, I approach the table. When I lock eyes with Tatum, her blue eyes plead with mine. We've always had a connection. Ever since we were kids, we could tell what the other was thinking with just a look. I know whatever is happening right now wasn't her doing.

Right before I reach the table, I clear my throat. My mom's head swivels toward me. "Is this an ambush or something?" With a hand on my waist, I pop my hip.

"Take a seat. There's no need to cause a scene." She pats the chair cushion next to her.

"If you didn't want a scene, you shouldn't have come."

I move past her and take the seat next to Tatum and directly across from my mom.

Tatum leans toward me and whispers, "I didn't invite her, she called me and when I said where I was going, she invited herself."

"It's okay. Would you expect anything else? This works better. We can clear the air." My gaze shoots to my mom. We pause and exchange glances before the server interrupts us to take our drink order.

Once the server is a few steps away from the table, Mom purses her red lips, leans in, and with her voice low she says, "Olivia, let's not do this here. Let's just have a nice lunch." She straightens in her seat and unfolds her napkin acting as if nothing's wrong. "How have you been?"

Any other person would be shocked by her sudden change of behavior, but not me. Sadly, I'm used to it. "I'm great. More than great actually."

"That's good to hear. We'll have to start making plans for the fall charity gala."

I rest my elbows on the table. "That's not going to work for me."

She flinches as if I smacked her across the face. "What do you mean? You always help with the charity galas."

With my chin raised, I say, "I'm starting my own event coordinating business."

"Olivia, that's amazing!" Tatum says.

"What do you know about starting a business?" my mom scoffs.

I roll my eyes at my mom's question and turn to Tatum. "I'm so excited. Hollyn and Van let me put fliers and business cards in their bakery, which led to a couple meetings to organize some birthday parties."

"I'm so proud of you, Olivia." Tatum wraps her arms around my shoulders and pulls me into a tight hug.

"Thanks." My gaze shoots back to my mom. "Ledger has been so supportive. He's the one who encouraged me to do what I'm passionate about."

She doesn't say anything, but instead subtly rolls her eyes. Over the years, she's perfected the casual eye roll. So much so, that to most people it would go unnoticed, but not me. I've seen her do it thousands of times. I won't let her get away with it this time.

"Instead of pretending we're a big happy family having lunch, let's address the giant elephant in the room" Heat creeps up my neck as rage and hurt course through my veins. "I'm the happiest I've ever been. To be honest, I didn't know what true happiness was until I stepped out from under your thumb. When I share that happiness with you, you squash it like a bug under your shoe." I tug my cardigan off and throw it over the back of my chair.

Tatum's eyes go wide along with my mom's. But hers are for a different reason. Tatum grabs my wrist to inspect my tattoo.

"When did you get this?" She runs her finger along the permanent ink.

I can't hide my smile. Every time I think of it, look at it, or talk about it, I think of Ledger. "Last week."

"Why a key?" Tatum asks.

"It's the key to Ledger's heart." My smile grows wider.

"Oh my God. That's so sweet." She continues to admire the tattoo.

The sour expression on my mom's face doesn't go unnoticed. She's never been a fan of tattoos. In fact, she despises them. But I didn't do it to defy her, I did it for me. But I won't lie, a thrill shoots through me knowing she hates it.

"Oh Olivia. I wish you wouldn't have defiled your body like that. You're too beautiful for that."

"So, I'm less beautiful because of it?"

"That's not what I said. Let's talk about something else."

"Okay. Let's get everything out on the table. No more lies. Why was Dad so adamant that I stop seeing Ledger?"

She rolls her head to the side. "Oh honey, it doesn't matter anymore."

"It matters to me."

She sighs. "The plan was for you to marry a man who held a lot of prestige in the community to help further his career. But instead you broke up with every guy you dated."

"You mean every guy you shoved at me?" I know I should be fuming. Rage-flip the table, if I could lift it. Instead, I feel nothing. I'm numb from anything that pertains to my father. Then it dawns on me. "He's been doing this all my life, and you've been helping him. Every time you would set me up with a guy, it was someone Dad picked, wasn't it?"

Her eyes shift away from mine. And that's all I need to know.

"I don't want to become you. I don't want to be manipulated into having false happiness. Ledger doesn't do that to me. He'll never do that to me."

She purses her lips and shakes her head. "You think you have it all figured out, but you don't know anything. Your father and I have a mutual arrangement that benefits the both of us."

"I don't want a marriage based on an arrangement. I want one based on love." Shoving my chair away from the table, I rise to my feet and glare down at my mom. "I'm done with this. All of this." I glance at my sister. "Call me later." Without saying another word, I stroll out of the restaurant with my head held high. I exorcised a few demons out of my life, just without all the spewing vomit. And now there's nothing but sunshine and rainbows in front of me. To any outsider, it would appear as if I had it all. There were times when I thought I did too, but I didn't realize I was actually drowning. And Ledger threw me the life preserver. Now, I want to see the man who puts this smile on my face.

# CHAPTER THIRTY-EIGHT

# THE BOMB

*Ledger*

When I arrive at the shop, Jay's hunched over in front of his tool bench having a staring contest with the mystery box.

"Who's winning?"

"Huh?" He turns to me.

"You or the box?" I nod at the small cardboard box sitting in front of him.

"I don't know, but you should find out what this is." He lifts the box and tosses it at me.

"What the hell, man?" I fumble with the box, careful so it doesn't crash to the ground as something inside shifts around.

"What if it's a bomb?"

"And you just threw it at me. Asshole." I lift the box to

my ear to listen if it's making a noise, and I give it a gentle shake.

"Bombs nowadays don't have ticking timers. You'll have to open it up to find out."

I glare at him as I shoulder past him, setting the box on the tool bench. Reaching for a box cutter, I run the blade down the taped flaps. They slowly pop open. I take a cautionary step back, holding my breath, waiting for something to happen.

Jay peeks over my shoulder. "Not a bomb."

I elbow him in the chest and he backs off, laughing. My attention returns to the box, I peel open the flaps and inside sits a folded piece of lined notebook paper. I reach inside to grab it, and then I see what's underneath. "Holy shit," I whisper.

"What? What is it?" Jay peers over my shoulder again.

"It's my phone. The one that went missing."

"What the fuck?"

Leaving the phone in the box, I unfold the note. I scan over the familiar handwriting.

*Ledge,*

*I'm sorry. I'm sorry for everything. But I'm mostly sorry for ruining things between us all those years ago. They say you never know what you've got until it's gone, and those words have never been truer.*

*When I came back to town this time, I was hoping things could have been different. We could be an us again, but you've moved on and I can't blame you. But when I found out you were with* someone else, I was hurt and I wasn't thinking straight.

John Ellis showed up at your house while you were at the shop. He knew who I was, and he figured out pretty quick that I was there for you. He offered me 10K to break you two up. One day at the shop, I was in your office snooping for anything and that's when I found your phone. When I opened it, because you've had the same password since you were seventeen, I found the pictures of Olivia. I thought if we could get Olivia to think you posted these photos, she would surely break up with you. I passed the info to John on a USB and he gave me the money.

Am I proud that I hurt you for money? No. But now I can start over. Somewhere new. I'm sorry. For everything. Have an amazing life. You deserve it.

Stevie

I bark out a laugh. This would surprise any other person, but not me. After everything that's happened, this makes perfect sense. Sometimes when life throws shit your way, all you can do is laugh.

"What does it say?" Jay asks. I hold the paper out to him, and he reads it. "Jesus Christ. All this shit for some money."

"Olivia's father was the puppet master and Stevie was the money hungry puppet." I grab the paper from Jay and toss it into the box with the phone. I'll have to show Olivia this later.

The rumble of a motorcycle engine echoes through the parking lot before coming to a halt in front of the open garage door. Archie steps off his bike and enters the garage. His expression is indifferent. I haven't seen or spoken to him since Stevie left. He comes to a stop in front of me. I hold out my hand for him to shake. He eyes it for a brief second before his firm grip clasps around mine. He wouldn't be shaking my hand if bad blood boiled between us.

Dropping my hand, I say, "Sorry for kicking Stevie out. I wish I didn't have to. I just couldn't deal with it anymore."

The creases on his forehead soften. "Nothing to be sorry about. Stevie told me what she did. I hope that didn't jeopardize what you have with your new girl."

I chuckle. "Oddly enough, it brought us closer together."

He nods. "Good to hear that. You deserve some happiness."

"How is she?"

"After she got the money, she does what she does best and left. I told her if she leaves not to come back. So, it's hard to say. Sometimes they need some tough love. Kinda like you." He clasps my shoulder.

"It wasn't tough love I needed. I just needed someone to care."

"You'll always be like a son to me. I'm partially to blame for this mess. A part of me hoped the longer you and Stevie were together, you two would work out your differences and make it work. So, I could call you my son."

I pull away from him. "You purposely took your time to come get her?" Rage bubbles up inside me as my fists clench. He doesn't say anything, but the regret in his eyes tells me it was only with good intentions. As much as I want, I can't be mad at him. "Look, me and Stevie have always been on two different paths. It was never going to work out. Plus, I have Olivia." My lips tip up into a smile as images of Olivia flip through my mind. Hell, I haven't ever smiled as much as I have since I've met her. It's a foreign feeling, but one I'm starting to enjoy.

"I'm happy for you." He pauses. "And I'm proud of what you've done."

I give him a nod. It hits differently when he tells me he's proud of me. Throughout my entire life, those were words I rarely heard. So, when they come from him, they have a little more meaning. A little bit of my anger toward him dissipates.

"Enough of this sappy bullshit. When do I get to meet this girl of yours?"

I laugh. "We'll have to plan something."

As if we've summoned her from heaven, Olivia's white SUV pulls into the parking lot and stops next to Archie's bike. She opens her door, steps out, and rounds the hood. She's wearing dark jeans and heels that accentuate her legs. Her blonde hair cascades down her shoulders and over a cream colored, chunky sweater. When our gazes meet, a wide smile lights up her face and I can't help giving her one of my own.

From beside me, Archie blows out a low whistle. "Is that her?"

Without breaking eye contact with Olivia, I nod. "It is." Before she can reach me, I close the distance between us. I grip the nape of her neck, hauling her to me in a bruising kiss. Keeping it short, I break away. "I love you."

Her eyes shine bright. "I love you too."

"Let me introduce you to someone." I intertwine my

fingers with hers, giving them a gentle squeeze. Turning around, we walk hand in hand, coming to a stop in front of Archie. "This is my girlfriend, Olivia. Olivia, this is Archie."

She holds out her hand. "It's so great to meet you. I've heard so much about you."

He grips hers in return. "Likewise." Without dropping her hand, he turns to me. "Better not fuck it up with this one."

A hearty laugh escapes me. "Alright, enough touching my girl." I swat his arm away and pull Olivia to my chest.

"Alright. Alright." Archie laughs. "I just wanted to stop by and let you know no hard feelings. But I'll let you get back to it."

He turns and makes his way to his bike, but I call out to him, halting his footsteps. "Archie!" He turns around. "Thanks for everything. We'll have to go for a ride soon."

He nods, then he's out of the garage and getting on his bike. Starting it up, he revs the engine, then he's out of the parking lot and pulling onto the street. The roar of the engine grows quieter until it's eventually swallowed up by the other traffic noise.

"You going to tell her about the box?" Jay asks as he leans against the tool bench, the box next him.

"Oh! The box from this morning?" Olivia's gaze flits to mine, then Jay's.

I nod and lead her to the tool bench. I pull open the top and pass her the note first. She unfolds the paper and we all sit in silence while she reads it.

"Wow. Let me get this straight. My father found out about Stevie and paid her ten thousand dollars to break us up. Which led her to stealing your phone, finding the pictures, and passing them along to frame you." Her gaze jumps to mine.

"That's what I've gathered."

"My father was on a mission to destroy us and he didn't care who he hurt in the process." She shakes her head. "But why did she come clean now?"

"I don't know. Felt guilty? She would never intentionally hurt me. I know that, but your dad found some low hanging fruit and took advantage. Apparently, it was too good of an offer for her to pass up." I don't hold a grudge against Stevie. Mostly, I want her to find her place in this world. It took me several years, but I know I've found mine.

"We can put everything behind us now. No more controlling parents. No more surprise ex-girlfriends?" She raises an eyebrow.

"We should be safe." I grip her cheeks with my palms, brushing my thumbs over her soft skin. Bending down, I press my lips to hers, loving the contrast of her softness against my hard edges.

"Ugh!" Jay groans from behind us. "Get a room!"

I break our kiss, but keep my hands pressed to her cheeks. "What do you say? Go to my office?"

"Sounds like an excellent idea." She beams up at me.

"Oh, look at that. It's lunchtime." Jay pushes off the tool bench and clasps my shoulder. "Text me when you're done." With that, he strolls out of the garage.

"I love you, duchess."

"And I love you, bad boy."

# TWO MONTHS LATER

## Olivia

I spin around, taking in my first large charity event. A parent from a kid's birthday party I organized asked me to plan an event their employer was hosting. I jumped at the chance. I've helped with so many charity events over the years, it thrilled me to finally organize one solo. All the late-night phone calls, last minute décor and catering changes were stressful, especially doing everything myself. But as I glance around at the blue and silver décor that drapes around the ballroom, I couldn't be happier with the way everything turned out. After the execution of several smaller successful events, I quit my job at The Blue Stone Group and started my own business. Ledger's been by my side, behind the scenes anyway, helping me and encouraging me every step of the way. If it wasn't for him, I wouldn't be earning a living doing something I love.

Ledger strolls toward me with a champagne flute in one hand and a low ball in the other. I wasn't able to convince him to buy a suit, but he compromised on black slacks and a white button down. I wanted to ask for a tie, but didn't want to push my luck. He's hotter like this, anyway. The collar hangs loose around his neck, showing off his tattoo. But my favorite part, his sleeves are rolled up to his elbows, his drool worthy forearms on full display. If anyone says forearms aren't sexy, they've never seen Ledger's. To top off his ensemble, his matte black combat boots. If we weren't in a room full of people, I would jump him right now. Instead, I'll show a little restraint, until we get home.

Every time I catch sight of his new tattoo, butterflies flutter in my belly. On the inside of his left wrist is an open padlock with *Duchess* filling the inside in a gothic script. After I told him why I got the key on my right wrist, he wanted the padlock on his left, for when we hold hands.

"Duchess, this place looks amazing." He hands the flute to me.

"Thanks. I'm happy with how everything turned out." I take a sip of the bubbly liquid.

"It looks almost as amazing as you." He wraps a hand around my waist, tugging me to him and pressing his lips to my forehead. You'd never expect the big, grumpy, bad boy would have a sweet and tender spot, but he's shown me everything. Times like this, in public, I love his sweet side, but when we're behind closed doors, I want the bad. This good girl will always crave my bad boy.

Trey strolls up to us with Mona and Kenny following close behind. "Look at us. One big happy family." Ledger glares at him, and I shake my head, but my smile is on full display. "What? Too soon?"

Mona slaps his arm. "Behave." Then she turns her attention toward me. "This place looks beautiful. But not quite as beautiful as you." She wraps her arms around me, hugging me tight.

"Thanks Mona. You're too kind."

When we break apart, she turns to Ledger. "Doesn't she look beautiful."

"Stunning." Ledger wraps his arm around my shoulder, tugging me to his chest.

While Trey and Ledger haven't become best friends, they've come to tolerate each other. They can at least be in the same room together without yelling expletives. I'll call that progress. But Ledger still likes to show off that I picked him over Trey by always touching me whenever Trey's near, like now. We've slowly eased back into family dinners. So far, no dinner rolls, or wine have been thrown.

Tatum walks into the ballroom, a pained expression on her face. I excuse myself from Ledger and Trey and pray they behave themselves.

I glide past groups of people until I'm in front of Tatum. Her eyes are puffy and red. "What's wrong? And don't tell me nothing."

She takes my hand in hers, pulling me to an empty table in the corner. She takes a seat and I do the same. Her gaze falls to the table. "Adam broke up with me. He said he needed to focus on his career."

"Career shameer. He's an idiot." I rest my hand on hers.

"But that's not the worst of it."

"What else did he do? Because I'll kill him. Or I'll have Ledger kill him. But I'll help bury the body."

She gives me a twinge of a smile. "He fired me. Well, his law firm said my position isn't needed at this time, but I know it was Adam's doing." Her shoulders drop and she wrings her hands together in her lap. A moment passes before she lifts her head. "I busted my ass to be the perfect girlfriend and the perfect administrative assistant and what do I get? Dumped and fired."

Seeing my sister like this breaks my heart. I never want to see her in pain and hurting. But then the wheels begin turning in my mind and my eyes light up.

"This is perfect!"

She flinches. "My life falling apart is … perfect?"

"Well, no, but also, it kinda is. Hear me out." I scoot to the edge of my chair.

"Yes, please explain this to me? Because right now, you're not making it sound very appealing."

"I'm sorry about Adam. He's a dumbass. You deserve someone who will cherish you and make you his top priority." I clasp her hands in mine. "But as for the job … Come work with me."

She lifts her head. Finally, a spark of interest fills her eyes. "As an event coordinator?"

"Yes! I have a big holiday event coming up for Christmas. Plus, I know how much you love Christmas. You always coordinate the Christmas decoration contest in your neighborhood. What do you say?"

Her bright red lips press together as she ponders my proposal. My toes bounce in my heels under the table as I anxiously wait for her answer. Working side by side with my sister would be amazing. More than amazing. It would be the best thing ever.

She turns to me, a wide grin spreads across her face and she nods. "Yes! Let's do it!"

I squeal in delight, wrapping Tatum in my arms. "This is going to be so fantastic! Let's go tell the guys."

Simultaneously, we rise to our feet, our faces breaking out into ear-to-ear grins. We make idle conversation as we glide across the polished marble floor of the ballroom. Suddenly, Tatum stops dead in her tracks. When I realize I'm talking to myself, I whirl around. She stares intently in front of her, her gaze never wavering. I follow the path and that's when I spot Adam embracing another girl tightly in his arms. It's not a sisterly embrace either. If I had to guess, he's imagining what she's wearing underneath her dress. I swiftly turn around to meet Tatum's gaze. Her face is a blank canvas, void of any emotion.

"That's his intern."

Thank you for reading Flirting with the Bad Boy! Want more Ledger and Olivia? Claim your copy of their fun and steamy bonus scene when you join my newsletter!

All Tatum wanted to do was immerse herself into the Christmas holiday and forget about being dumped. That is

273

until a sexy, grumpy musician moves in next door causing her tinsel to tie into knots. As she chips away at his icy facade she discovers she's falling for the Scrooge, but their time together might be shorter than she expected. Pick up your copy of Flirting with the Scrooge today!

If you enjoyed *Flirting with the Bad Boy*, I would love it if you let your friends know so they can also experience Ledger and Olivia's fun and exhilarating relationship as they find their happily ever after. If you leave a review for *Flirting with the Bad Boy* on the site from which you purchased the book, Goodreads, BookBub, or your own blog, I would love to read it. Feel free to email me the link at gia@authorgiastevens.com

You can stay up-to-date on upcoming releases and sales by joining my reader group or following me on social media.
Gia Stevens' Sassy Romance Readers
Facebook
Instagram

ACKNOWLEDGMENTS

First and foremost, I want to thank everyone who picked up this book. I think I will forever be in awe that you want to read my stories.

I have to thank my husband. I don't know if I would have ever started writing without his words of encouragement.

A big shout out to Brandi Zelenka. You were there for me every step of the way and I don't think I could have done this without you.

To my creative team, you pushed me to put out the best book possible and I am so thankful to have you on my side. Thank you to my editor, Brandi at My Notes in the Margin. I tend to give you a hot mess and you make it brilliant.

Thank you to Katy Cuthbertson for all your work and support, especially your eye for commas. You've been a huge help.

Thank you to my beta readers Jessie Bailey, and Randi Gauthreaux. You gave me invaluable feedback to help make my manuscript sparkle. Thank you to my proofreader Tonya Fender. You've helped me out so much.

Thank you Enticing Journey Book Promotions for your amazing PR work. You made everything run smoothly.

Most of all thank you to all the bloggers, bookstagrammers, and booktokers for reading and sharing your excitement for this book. It means the world to me and I can't thank you enough. And of course, thank you to all the readers for reading my words. I hope I've been able to give you a fun escape for a few hours.

See you at the next book! Stay sassy!

Gia Stevens resides in Northern Minnesota with her husband and cat, Smokey. She lives for the warm, sunny days of summer and dreads the bitter cold of winter. A romantic comedy junkie at heart, she knew she wanted her own stories to encompass those same warm and fuzzy feelings.

When she's not busy writing your next book boyfriend, Gia can be found binge watching TV shows that aired five years ago, taking pictures of her cat, or curled up with a smutty book.

ALSO BY GIA STEVENS

Want to read more sassy heroines, swoony heroes, and fun and flirty romance books?

Visit Gia's website to find a complete list of all her books.

Printed in Great Britain
by Amazon